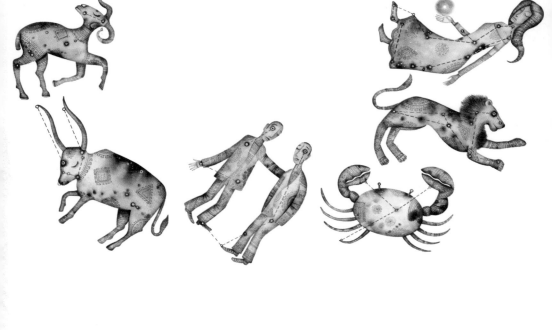

ASTRO
THERAPY

Other Schiffer Books on Related Subjects:
The Beginner's Guide to Astrology: Class Is in Session,
Dusty Bunker, ISBN 978-0-7643-5330-7
Claiming Your Power through Astrology: A Spiritual Workbook,
Emily Klintworth, ISBN 978-0-7643-5272-0

Illustrations and interior photographs: iStock
Cover illustration: Shutterstock

© First published in French by Mango, Paris, France--2018
Original title in French: Astro-thérapie
The publisher would like to thank Alexandra Rousselle for her
valuable and effective assistance.

Despite all the care taken in editing this book and checking the
internet links mentioned, the publisher does not host the URL
links indicated on p. 158 and cannot therefore guarantee their
durability.

Type set in Bell Gothic/ Amplitude

ISBN: 978-0-7643-6074-9
Printed in China

Published by Red Feather Mind, Body, Spirit
An imprint of Schiffer Publishing, Ltd.
4880 Lower Valley Road
Atglen, PA 19310
Phone: (610) 593-1777; Fax: (610) 593-2002
E-mail: Info@schifferbooks.com
Web: www.redfeathermbs.com

For our complete selection of fine books on this and related
subjects, please visit our website at www.schifferbooks.com.
You may also write for a free catalog.

ASTRO
THERAPY

Discover how to live better and move forward in life with your astral theme

PHILIPPE REGNICOLI

REDFeather™

MIND | BODY | SPIRIT

4880 Lower Valley Road, Atglen, PA 19310

CONTENTS

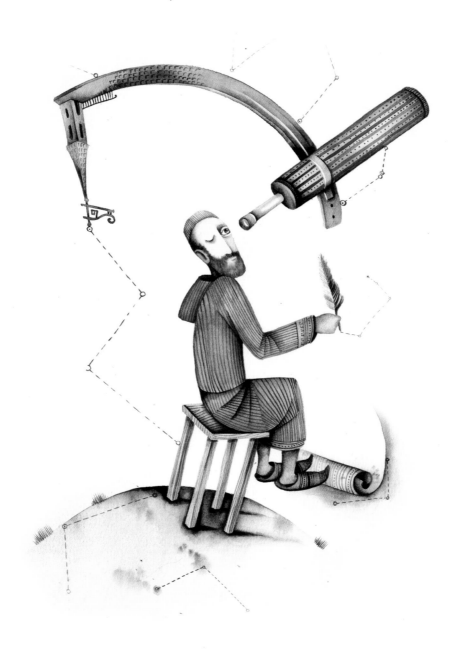

INTRO-
DUCTION

INTRODUCTION

It is difficult to date the beginning of astrological practice. Its birth is confused with the first observations of the sky, the development of the first calendars (solar or lunar), the erection of buildings resolutely oriented toward the sky (the pyramids, Stonehenge, etc.), and, of course, the initial observations establishing the complex relationships that link the sky and the Earth, starting with the influence of the Moon on nature, fauna, flora, and human beings. Astrology is a tool that has evolved along with human societies. If, for safety's sake, we adopt the most recent dating, we are sure that the first astronomy tables (called ephemerides) used to draw up a horoscope (also called a sky chart, birth chart, or even astrological wheel) are at least 2,500 years old (the inhabitants of Sumer and Babylon knew how to anticipate astral movements as early as the 5th century BCE).

It can be said that astrology is then essentially naturalistic, since for the moment it is a question of establishing relevant correlations (in the form of cause-and-effect links) between what happens astronomically and what happens in nature, about the climate, animals, epidemics, etc.

Very quickly, however, astrology (which has always evolved over time) became enriched by advances in mathematics, geometry, and astronomy, soaking up the wisdom of Greek philosophy in the process (notably that of Aristotle, who taught that everything that lives and dies depends on the "movements of the higher world").

Thus, astrology gained weight, and traces of individual horoscopes as early as 410 BCE have been found, evidence that astrology was already used for personal purposes even if it remained for a long time the prerogative of the elite (in particular, kings, princes, and high dignitaries).

Resisting the pressures of religious power and then scientific revolutions (such as heliocentrism), astrology grew century after century, using, for example, statistics (e.g., Paul Choisnard) or incorporating psychoanalytical data (e.g., André Barbault).

It can be said that the twentieth century was the century of the democratization of astrology, which, thanks in particular to the publication of many books and specialized journals, can now be transmitted on a large scale.

As for the evolution of astrology over the last four decades, it leads us directly to the subject of our book, since it is with the New Age movement that astrology resolutely became a tool for personal development (i.e., a set of techniques and advice aimed at unleashing the full potential of each individual), thus enabling him to optimize both his life and his happiness. It is highly representative that the book that theorized the New Age (and which brought together many spiritual domains) is titled *The Aquarian Conspiracy* (written by the psychologist Marilyn Ferguson in 1980).

THE ADVANTAGES OF ASTROLOGY IN PERSONAL DEVELOPMENT

Despite the emergence each year of new methods of personal development astrology (NLP, relaxation therapy, EMDR, etc.), this grand dame, over three thousand years old, remains the unseated champion in the universe for helping one to know oneself. Quite simply because its basic premise is not to propose a general method applicable to all (as philosophy, for example, can do), but to offer personalized advice according to each individual. Astrology is entirely based on the idea that each person is a unique microcosm and that there is no prescription for happiness applicable to everyone, in any situation, and at any time. Its very support (the birth chart) is a representation of an individual's singularity.

In fact, a simple calculation (but with an "astronomical" result!) will shed light on the richness contained in astrology: there are twelve signs of the zodiac. Our system includes two luminaries (the Sun and the Moon), seven planets (Mercury, Venus, Mars, Jupiter, Saturn, Uranus, and Neptune), and two dwarf planets (Ceres and Pluto), or eleven main astral bodies. The zodiac wheel is divided into twelve distinct sectors (or houses) that vary according to location and date of birth (including time). If we take these basic elements, we already arrive at 1,584 possible combinations (and therefore different individualities).

To the astrologer must be added dozens of other elements, such as fictitious points (such as the nodal axis or the black moon) or certain stars of great magnitude.

Since planets move at varying speeds, it literally takes thousands of years for a planetary configuration to reproduce exactly (i.e., even if some factors may be common to several themes, the total arrangement of these factors will not be the same). Therefore, in astrology there isn't a SINGLE model that we try to place on each one, but an infinite number of models that the astrologer seeks to understand in their subtle originality.

In a word, astrology recognizes, and even defends, the fact that each of us is different. This difference is our wealth and strength. Denying it is our misfortune; taking it in charge, accepting it, and developing it allows us to fulfill the unique role we play in our family, our society, and our universe. Only in this way can we flourish.

TWO DIFFERENT WAYS TO READ
THIS BOOK

The following pages will refer to many astrological notions, and there are two ways to approach them: the first is to have your own theme and to be able to refer to it whenever necessary, which is the analytical method; the second is to rely on your intuition: that is, to read all the given definitions and find the one that speaks most to you, which corresponds most to you. This is the intuitive method.

Many websites allow you to obtain your sky chart (some even offer interpretations automatically generated by software, which we invite you to be wary of). There are also many software programs (including free ones) to generate birth charts (type in your search engine the keywords "free astrology software").

Here are some basics for recognizing astrological data on a theme if you are a novice:

■ First of all, **the abbreviations of the signs** that you may find useful:

■ AR for Aries
■ TAU or TA for Taurus
■ GEM or GM or GE for Gemini
■ CAN or CN for Cancer
■ LE for Leo
■ VIR or VI or VR for Virgo
■ LI for Libra

- SCO or SC for Scorpio
- SAG or SG for Sagittarius
- CAP or CP for Capricorn
- AQUA or AQ for Aquarius
- PIS or PI for Pisces

- Then, there are the symbols frequently used for the signs:

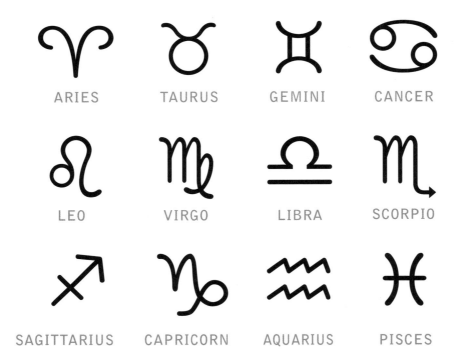

ARIES	TAURUS	GEMINI	CANCER
LEO	VIRGO	LIBRA	SCORPIO
SAGITTARIUS	CAPRICORN	AQUARIUS	PISCES

If you see a reference of the type "16[letters]5" (for example, "16CAP5" or "13[symbol drawn]16"), it means that the number before the letters or symbol indicates the degree. The letters or symbol used indicates the sign. For example, 07TAU15 means that the astrological point of interest to you is at 07°15' from the sign of Taurus.

To use the analytical method, you need to know only the position in the astral chart of the planets and astrological elements that will be discussed: their meaning and interpretation are explained in this book.

■ Finally, the **symbols of the planets and dynamic points:**

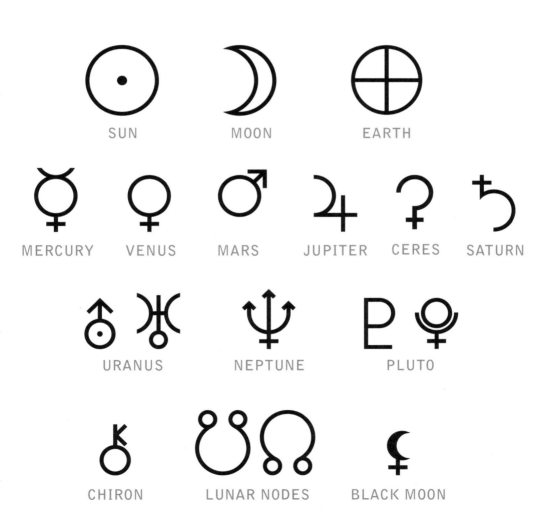

SUN   MOON   EARTH

MERCURY   VENUS   MARS   JUPITER   CERES   SATURN

URANUS   NEPTUNE   PLUTO

CHIRON   LUNAR NODES   BLACK MOON

TEST: DETERMINE YOUR ASTROLOGICAL DOMINANT

A professional astrologer can easily determine your dominant; it is one of the first things he usually does because, as its name suggests, this dominant is what seems to mark your character and your life the most; therefore what is important to you. Otherwise, there is an intuitive method of answering the next test as truthfully as possible.

For each question, assign a score of 0 to 2 depending on your level of agreement with the proposal:

0 = No / not really / not at all
1 = Sometimes / it all depends / it's partly true
2 = Generally yes / I agree / close to the truth

Count the points and identify the three letters with the highest score. Each letter corresponds to an astrological dominant (a sign and an element). The one with the highest score is your first dominant (the conductor of your birth sky, in a way), and the next two are your codominants, sort of assistants.

> **NOTE**
> Don't be surprised if your dominants are different from your sign or ascendant—that's what makes it all the more interesting!

QUESTIONS

■ I easily feel attacked when I am contradicted.   A: ....

■ I have a slow working pace; I don't like to be rushed.   B: ....

■ It is important to have a role in life.   E: ....

■ Giving meaning to your life is the
  most important thing.   I: ....

■ I enjoy physical activity and competition in general.   A: ....

■ I need to feel materially safe.   B: ....

■ I like to meet new people.   C: ....

■ I like to take time to remember or dream.   D: ....

■ I am considered to be "a resourceful person."   K: ....

■ All my actions are carefully thought out, planned.   F: ....

■ I spend a lot of energy convincing others.   I: ....

■ I always have at least one project in
  mind for the future.   K: ....

■ I don't take initiatives without consulting others.   G: ....

■ Life without sex is like a dish without spices.   H: ....

■ Sometimes I delude myself or idealize
  things and people.   L: ....

■ I like beginnings more than routine.   A: ....

■ I seek peace above all else.   G: ....

■ I often wait until the last minute to do things.   K: ....

■ I fall in love easily, but it doesn't last.   A: ....

■ I would have liked (or like) to have a great
loving family.   D: ....

■ Sometimes I'm self-destructive.   H: ....

■ I can't stand hierarchy.   K: ....

■ I am very influenced by people's moods.   L: ....

■ I like to win in individual challenges.   A: ....

■ I'm more of a homebody.   D: ....

■ Any truth is good to tell, even when it hurts.   H: ....

■ I have trouble expressing my emotions but
not my ideas.   J: ....

■ Having faith in something is the only driving
force in life.   L: ....

■ To solve a problem, you need as much information
as possible.   C: ....

■ I let my naturalness speak for itself and I easily
show my emotions.   D: ....

■ Reason must prevail over emotion.   F: ....

■ I try to find the right balance in everything.   G: ....

■ Challenges motivate me.   H: ....

■ I have principles and I stick to them.   J: ....

■ Sometimes I have genius ideas.   K: ....

■ I have the ability to "take everything on
  my shoulders."   L: ....

■ I know how to comfort people, how to bring
  them warmth.   E: ....

■ Being socially integrated is the most
  important thing.   F: ....

■ I like to debate, but I don't like to argue.   G: ....

■ I'm ready to start over if necessary.   H: ....

■ I am happy to take the others under my
  protective wing.   I: ....

■ You have to know how to take responsibility
  for your actions.   J: ....

■ I don't think we know everything about the
  mysteries of the universe.   L: ....

■ My reactions are often thoughtless,
  sometimes aggressive.   A: ....

■ I accumulate grievances and then I explode.   B: ....

■ It's rare that I don't go out during the day.   C: ....

■ I judge things by how I feel and my impressions.   D: ....

- I am charismatic and generous.   E: ....

- I don't like to impose myself, and I'm good at sorting things out.   G: ....

- Regular change is part of life; it is even vital.   H: ....

- Being alone doesn't bother me.   J: ....

- When I love someone, I feel in osmosis with him.   L: ....

- I like to launch ideas and projects.   A: ....

- Eating well is part of life's pleasures.   B: ....

- I always try to take the opinions of others into account.   C: ....

- To be happy, I need to be able to dream.   D: ....

- You mustn't play on my susceptibility or be disrespectful.   E: ....

- I always try to measure my abilities.   F: ....

- I am known for my kindness and joviality.   I: ....

- Unhappy people are those who have no ambition.   J: ....

- I love understanding how things work.   K: ....

- My sensuality is strong and healthy.   B: ....

- I talk a lot, just for the pleasure of chatting.   C: ....

- I'm very expressive.   D: ....

- I have already experienced passion several times.   E: ....

- I have complexes but I'm taking care of myself.   F: ....

- I question myself and try to improve myself.   H: ....

- I often trust fate and my lucky star.   I: ....

- The opinions of experienced people should
be respected.   J: ....

- I feel empathy for others.   L: ....

- I alternate effort and comfort, work and idleness.   B: ....

- I like to have several activities or projects
at the same time.   C: ....

- I naturally take the role of leader or as an organizer.   E: ....

- I need order and a certain routine to avoid stress.   F: ....

- Indecision is one of my main handicaps.   G: ....

- I like to pass on what I have learned.   I: ....

- I am cautious, pragmatic, and persevering.   J: ....

- They say I am reassuring, solid, and warm.   B: ....

- I'm a natural player.   C: ....

- I like to create; I even need it.   E: ....

- I am diligent, careful, and methodical.   F: ....

- Living alone is the most depressing thing there is.   G: ....

- I am said to be tolerant, cheerful, and charitable.   I: ....

- I am proud of my originality.   K: ....

20

A: ....

B: ....

C: ....

D: ....

E: ....

F: ....

G: ....

H: ....

I: ....

J: ....

K: ....

L: ....

RESULTS

■ If you have mostly **A**, your dominant is Aries
and your element is Fire. Your planet is Mars.

■ If you have mostly **B**, your dominant is Taurus
and your element is the Earth. Your planet is Venus.

■ If you have mostly **C**, your dominant is Gemini
and your element is the Air. Your planet is Mercury.

■ If you have mostly **D,** your dominant is Cancer
and your element is Water. Your planet is the Moon.

■ If you have mostly **E**, your dominant is Leo
and your element is Fire. Your planet is the Sun.

■ If you have mostly **F**, your dominant is Virgo
and your element is the Earth. Your planet is Ceres.

■ If you have mostly **G**, your dominant is Libra
and your element is the Air. Your planet is Venus.

■ If you have mostly **H,** your dominant is Scorpio
and your element is Water. Your planet is Pluto.

■ If you have mostly **I**, your dominant is Sagittarius
and your element is Fire. Your planet is Jupiter.

■ If you have mostly **J**, your dominant is Capricorn
and your element is the Earth. Your planet is Saturn.

■ If you have mostly **K,** your dominant is Aquarius
and your element is the Air. Your planet is Uranus.

■ If you have mostly **L**, your dominant is Pisces
and your element is Water. Your planet is Neptune.

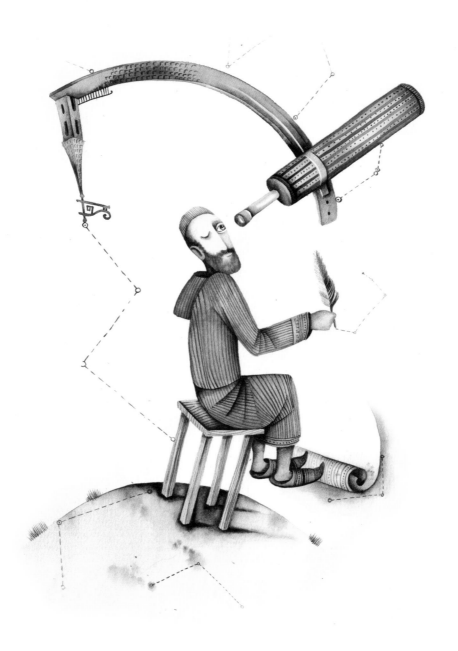

WHO
AM I?

AN ORIGINAL SELF

Astrology is not a belief, much less a religion or an esoteric practice. It is a discipline of the mind, a study of the human psyche, and, in this sense, a true psychology.

An observation of the essential

One of the greatest services that astrology can provide us is to help us see the deep essence of our being, beyond the educational and social veneer that coats us. Thus, we can focus on our true nature, which gives us strength (because we are reconnected to our source) to face what has to be.

Although we don't intend to revive the eternal debate between the innate and what is learned, it must be noted (and it is enough to let early-childhood professionals testify to convince yourself of this) that each of us has, from birth, a different temperament from our neighbor and our parents. It is very rare that children are "as they are raised," unless education could have promoted a potential that already existed. The environment and genes have a certain influence but do not explain everything. Thanks to the tools of astrology, we can examine another influence (that one could qualify as a mystical cause, for ease of reference) by establishing an astrological theme.

An astrological reading is not fixed

A theme is very rarely 100 percent accurate, since part of our birth potential (about 10%–15%) has never been updated and has been blocked by circumstances—education, social, national, etc. (in short, a number of external factors that need to be taken into account).

In addition, each person (fortunately) is constantly evolving: some traits of youth may disappear while others will appear over time. The theme therefore represents the overall potentials we have at birth, but cannot be a definitive snapshot of our personality since we remain free to change, to arrange, to work on ourselves.

It is also interesting to see which native potentials are minimal or not developed at all, because this is often an indication of a blockage (psychological, educational) that it is a good idea to work on in order to release energies.

The rediscovery of an admirable potential

Not only can the astrological tool help us perceive our essential nature, but once this is done, it can also allow us to fully deploy it, which in itself constitutes a possibility of inner harmonization and fortification.

Even better: by revealing who we are deeply, astrology restores our dignity as human beings and allows us to better understand the meaning of our coming into the world and the role we have to play in it. Thanks to it, we can conceive ourselves as an element (singular and important) of a great whole, essential to the proper functioning of the whole. If this element is "broken" or sick, if it does not work as it should, then the whole universe is sick and does not work as it should . . .

Astrology therefore contains the idea that every human being is infinitely precious, that he has his place in the world, and that, provided he escapes corrupting influences, this place is necessarily positive. It is enough to observe children's joy in simply living (discovering, playing, learning to talk, learning to do . . .) to understand that life is complicated and difficult only because it is made complex. Astrology is also a return to the simplest part of the human being: his cosmic nature, first, universal.

Astrology, a tool for liberation

The astrological approach aims to allow everyone to live better according to his interior nature while being in harmony with the cosmos. Of being able to choose the possibility of being the person that best suits us. It is our innate inclination, the one that allows us to function healthfully (as opposed to toxic behavior that we adopt under external pressure and constraints).

It is also a question of restoring not only the sacred relationship that exists between each individual and others, but also between each individual and the world, the *spiritus mundi*. By getting to know and respect each other better, respect for difference will follow spontaneously: one of the obvious riches of astrology is to offer us several thousand different human models and thus to emphasize that variety is the norm, while conformity makes us miserable.

In astrology, everyone has their own personality and mission. No one is to be excluded, since each birth can be seen as a "reflection of the universe" at a given time. Who could conceive of rejecting or despising a portion of Time?

> *You are perfect as you are . . .*
> *But there is still room for improvement!*
> —Shunryu Suzuki (Zen master)

This perception of the cosmic nature of Man is not a way of ignoring or fleeing from social reality, everyday life and the need for everyone to make an effort, quite the contrary! However, it is only by regaining self-esteem that we can fully become part of a couple and define our role in our family, our society...

What is your dominant state of life?

One could summarize by saying that the purpose of astrology as a tool for personal development is to reach its full potential. Nevertheless, as has been suggested, this goal is not achieved without effort; this potential is not given to us from the outset.

Explaining the causes of this basic imperfection would lead to debates that have no place here, but we can at least retain the general idea that the very reason for our presence on Earth as human beings is to improve ourselves. We ALL come with our challenges (e.g., becoming autonomous people or developing our sensitivity) and weaknesses (e.g., greed or anger). So, one of the main obstacles that astrology can help us identify and overcome is our existential dynamic, or the state of life that initially dominates us.

This dominant state of life is directly related to our dominant elemental (i.e., the astrological element that dominates in the birth chart; see p. 11). There are four main categories (active/choleric, pragmatic/scared, sociable/unstable, and imaginative/ sad), and each of us obviously fits into one of them, although it is neither surprising nor rare to be a combination of two or even three states that cohabit and succeed each other. Each state of life has its positive and negative sides.

We will first read the elemental dominant that corresponds to our first astrological dominant (for example, Fire if your first dominant is Aries, and Water if it is Cancer), but we will also be able to read the two codominants with profit, knowing that their influences will be secondary, less strong, or less frequent.

Dominant state of life: active/choleric

If you have a Fire dominant (or codominant), your dominant state of life is active/choleric.

An enthusiastic, determined, and dynamic person, always in action or reaction, you generally have self-confidence and pride, a sense of honor, and competition.

Often honest and spontaneous, you want to be able to freely express your deep essence (who you are), your creativity (what you imagine), and your vision of the world (what you think). However, you may lack tact, sensitivity and self-control, letting yourself get into states between irritability and anger. You often suffer from chronic impatience and easily sink into excess.

You are a fighter (you can fight against boredom, injustice, banality, etc.), but you are also authoritarian, while refusing yourself any submission.

Claiming a strong character, you often confuse the line between good or misplaced pride. Your pride creates certain aggressiveness but also allows you to advance in life with courage.

People quickly notice you (you act in this way), and your explosive nature makes some people admire you, while others fear you. You have a strong need for recognition and love.

YOUR CHALLENGE: to preserve your combative energy without becoming aggressive. To do this, give up your desire to dominate, to be the best, the first, the most loved, etc.; you will be truly appreciated and your great human qualities (warmth, generosity, chivalry) will be expressed in the best possible way. Ideally, apply your strength to the service of a noble cause where you will find your best social role.

Dominant state of life: pragmatic/fearful

If you have an Earth dominant (or codominant), your dominant state of life is pragmatic/worried.

Your reasoning is based on your senses . . . and your common sense. By striving for reason and realism, you become pragmatic and realize what is important to you.

Inspiration, creativity, and theory are certainly beautiful things, but, from your point of view, they are useless if they aren't inscribed in the real world, if we don't give them substance.

You have the patience, perseverance, and self-discipline to carry out your ideas (or those of others); it is more important for you to build than to think in a vacuum.

You are reputed to be enduring and faithful to your objectives as well as your loves, sometimes to the point of obstinacy or obsession, and it is rare to see you give up, lose hope, or stop along the way. You are hardworking as well as careful.

You must be careful to keep an open mind (especially concerning the invisible, but also by stopping being suspicious of everyone and withdrawing into yourself), and not to lock yourself into a routine or the ultraconventional.

You have a strong need for security (emotionally, materially, and socially).

YOUR CHALLENGE: to preserve realism and practical skills while accepting the part of the unknown and uncontrollable that any existence entails, so that you do not live constantly in fear (of loss, ruin, breakup, dismissal, etc.). An excessive need for certainty and security actually limits your daily life and will cause you to miss opportunities if you do not put them into perspective.

Dominant state of life: sociable/unstable

If you have an Air dominant (or codominant), your dominant state of life is sociable/unstable.

Your priority in life is ideas and encounters, the life of the mind. Giving importance to reflection, dialogue, theory, and concepts, you are comfortable with words, reasoning, and communication.

Sociable, loving to talk about everything and nothing, and capable of objectivity, you are not often in harmony with your body, finding instincts, emotions, and matter "cumbersome."

With your sociable humor, you are curious and interested in a variety of subjects; you enjoy chatting, walking, group activities, and combining your strengths and ideas with those of others.

Requiring a lot of stimulation, you easily find yourself lacking motivation (if your relational environment is not stimulating enough) or being torn between several directions (because you have the temptation to follow everyone).

Of course, you don't often get worked up, but beware of too much thoughtlessness or attachment to outer appearances in detriment to the contents: not all that glitters is gold!

You have a strong need for human contact and mental solicitation.

YOUR CHALLENGE: to preserve your smile and your ability to link knowledge while avoiding superficiality and instability.

It will always be beneficial for you to take the time to deepen things (and relationships with people) rather than to forage around. Also try to develop your empathy by sometimes silencing the constant stream of thoughts that agitate you; meditation will help you in this.

Dominant state of life: imaginative/sad

If you have a Water dominant (or codominant), your dominant state of life is imaginative/sad.

Sentimental and emotional, your inner life is of central importance, and you are always trying to bring your feelings and the outside world into harmony.

Able to let go when you are in love (you know all about mad passion . . .), you have a natural predisposition to rise above the contingencies of matter and daily life, through art, philosophy, faith, or authentic dedication to others.

Driven by powerful unconscious impulses, sometimes literally, and feeling carried away by your inner impulses (or an invisible power), you are very intuitive, inspired, and creative.

You are also very receptive; be careful not to let your emotions overwhelm you (starting with fear)—your hypersensitivity can cause you to have serial emotional shocks.

You are adaptable and flexible—it is difficult to identify you, let alone hold you back, unless your feelings push you to do so (and you then become rather susceptible to influence). It will therefore be necessary to choose your surroundings carefully, because you will otherwise easily fall into melancholy, or even depression.

You have a strong need for calm, protection, gentleness.

YOUR CHALLENGE: to preserve your sensitivity while still being able to face the world.

You must understand that joy depends not only on your environment but also on your vision of things. Developing a strong spirituality will prevent you from resigning yourself to the mundane. Surround yourself with positive people and don't judge yourself too harshly.

Me and self-awareness

It is not all about being, but it is also about being aware of who you are, which implies a sufficient distance from yourself.

How does our consciousness work? Isn't it intriguing that, very often, the image reflected in our mirror is not the one we see in our mind's eye? That is, there seems to be a sometimes-abyssal gap between our objective external existence (our body, our real skills) and our subjective inner existence (our "soul," our potentialities).

In astrology, this distance between what we are and what we perceive has always been taken into account. It is reflected in the presence of an astral factor representing the self (the Sun), and another representing consciousness and senses (Mercury). In the astrological theme, Mercury thus informs us about our vision of the world and ourselves.

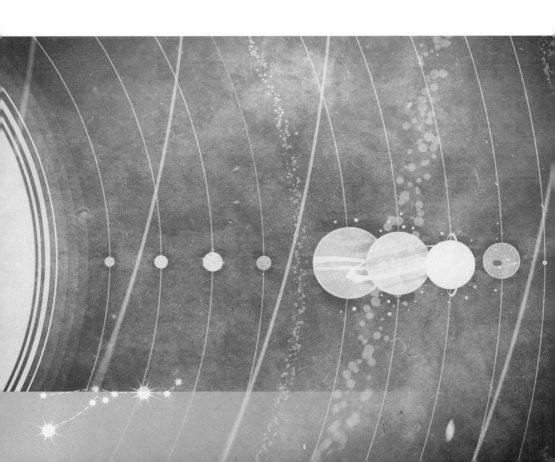

EXAMPLE

With his Mercury in Aries, Patrick tends to see the world and himself in terms of competition: he feels valued in moments of victory, of conquest.

To enrich his vision and not lose his self-esteem as soon as he encounters failure (which always ends up happening in a lifetime), it is important that in his process of personal development, Patrick also learns to assert himself more gently, through the expression of his tastes, values, and feelings rather than just in terms of confrontations and results.

The astrologer will also be able to help his consultant by asking whether Mercury is in the same sign as or different from the Sun, because if this is the case, he may lack objectivity, but there will be a natural harmony between his way of being and his vision of himself.

On the contrary, if Mercury and the Sun are in different signs, there is more objectivity, a sharper and critical idea of oneself, and greater chances of judging oneself too harshly, because our way of perceiving the world and our way of being are not, in an innate way, in unison. It will be important, therefore, to learn how to bring them together and make them work together.

EXAMPLE

With her Mercury in Libra and her Sun in Scorpio, Natasha perceives the world through the filter of feelings; she sees herself essentially through the relational network to which she belongs, and tends to assimilate with the people she associates with, seeking approval to preserve harmony.

However, her profound nature requires debates and challenges to prove that she really exists.

In her case, systematically fleeing confrontation cultivates external harmony at the price of her inner authenticity, which can't be satisfactory. In her process of personal development, it will therefore be good for her to understand that an opinion can be challenged without her arguing with the person issuing it; disagreeing intellectually does not mean rejecting each other emotionally.

Taking a step back: Planetary downshifts

There are methods in astrology that allow us to step back from our problems and choices we are confronted with. Among these methods, some belong to dynamic astrology, because it is necessary to specify that in addition to the observation of the sky at birth (so-called static astrology), one must take into account the movement of planets throughout life and the relationship that these movements (called transits) have with the natal chart. We then compare the factors of the birth chart—which do not vary—with the ever-changing position of the planets, which move endlessly in space. If we were to compare the course of the planets to a movie, the birth chart would be like a freeze frame. As we will see, comparing the still image and the rest of the film will teach us a lot.

NOTE:
There are two astrological techniques: static astrology, which studies the birth sky, and dynamic astrology, which studies the evolution of the birth sky in relation to current or future transits.

At times, a planet can retrograde (i.e., when observed from Earth, it appears that the planet's course is reversed and goes backward).

This astronomical phenomenon is easily identifiable through ephemerides (specialized astronomical tables), but its proper interpretation is difficult. Indeed, every human being is affected by retrogression, but differently according to his birth chart. Like any transit, it therefore takes a great deal of experience to explain its meaning properly: transit (whatever it may be) is, in a way, a universal emission, but each human being will be a particular receiver, integrating information differently.

By identifying retrogressions (emission) and placing them in the context of a person's native sky (the receiver), the astrologer can identify privileged periods to work on himself, to advance quickly in his inner journey. It is not enough to have the will to progress, but it is also necessary to know how to do it at the most-appropriate times!

The nature of the possible advances will depend on the nature of the planet that is retrogressing (Mercury, Venus, Mars, etc.), while the field in which the work of understanding is carried out will depend on the sector where this retrogression takes place in the individual theme.

Mercury's retrogressions are particularly valuable since this planet largely governs our perceptions and our thoughts.

When Mercury retrogresses, it is therefore a good time to think intensely, to review our points of view, to question our opinions, and to try to see things or people differently (including ourselves), from another angle.

This type of transit will help you develop great awareness; real inner evolutions and important fundamental work can then be done, especially if you are accompanied.

WHEN MERCURY RETROGRESSES

In order for you to be more attentive during these periods, here are Mercury's next retrogressions:

- From October 13 to November 3, 2020
- From January 30 to February 20, 2021
- From May 29 to June 22, 2021
- From September 27 to October 18, 2021
- From January 14 to February 3, 2022
- From May 10 to June 2, 2022
- From September 9 to October 2, 2022
- From December 29 to January 18, 2022

Depending on your theme, these retrogressions will affect some level of your life (emotional, professional, family, material, friendly, etc.) and will deliver a different message, but in any case, these periods will be particularly appropriate moments to think and acquire more lucidity in relation to yourself.

IS MY "SELF" COMPATIBLE WITH THE "OTHER"?

From an astrological perspective, each sign of the zodiac wheel is complementary to all the others.

The coherence of the zodiac

All the signs, and therefore everyone born under these different signs, are thus "interconnected" within a complex underlying network in which each has his place as an isolated unit (the individual) and his role as a connected unit (let us say the citizen, the word here being taken in the widest possible sense of "one who takes part in public life").

There is much to say about this internal coherence of the zodiac, but we can briefly summarize by saying that Aries initiates things, Taurus builds them, Gemini diversifies them, Cancer stabilizes them, Leo directs them, Virgo refines them, Libra shares them, Scorpio transforms them, Sagittarius enlarges them, Capricorn perpetuates them, Aquarius renews them, and Pisces raises them, transcends them.

Some signs of the zodiac (and therefore some psychological profiles) are said to be opposed, others in harmony, others still in succession or in tension (see the next paragraph on this subject). But each one of them is in fact essential to the functioning of the whole. In addition, a person sending us an inverted image, making us feel good about our feelings and ourselves, or, on the contrary, questioning our certainties, is a fundamental element of our own evolution and the right balance of the world. This means, and it is essential to understand this, that each of us is an important being for everyone else, irreplaceable because we are unique (and we know that what is rare is precious . . .).

By fully recognizing this, not only will we love each other more, but we will also respect others more, understanding that those who are different from us (including annoying people or heartbreakers) participate fully in the natural order of the world.

INDRA'S NET

It is a Hindu metaphor in which each being is considered as a gemstone locked in a gangue of vulgar rock. Indra's Net (King of the Gods and Lord of Heaven) is the world of men, the Earth. However, caught in the mesh of the net (i.e., incarnated in the form of flesh), precious stones, by rubbing against each other (through contact with others—sometimes brief, sometimes gentle) get rid of the vulgar rock that covers them, and end up shining brightly.

This mythological tale teaches us that only by living others allows us to reveal our full potential.

What is your best role in society?

As before (concerning the state of life), you will refer to the dominants to discover your best role in society. You will first read the elemental dominant that corresponds to your first astrological dominant (for example, Fire if your first dominant is Aries, and Water if it is Cancer), but you will also be able to read the two that correspond to your codominants, knowing that their influences will be more secondary, less strong, or less frequent.

Fire dominant (or codominant)

If you have a Fire dominant (or codominant), your best place in society is that of the guide, whether in the form of a pioneer, leader, or mentor.

You are full of desires and ideas! It is time to roll up your sleeves: convincing, ordering, or leading a group doesn't scare you. You want to do things, shape things—to act—and you can be very stimulating, dynamic, and voluntary in this sense.

Often naturally charismatic, you are driven by an ideal, a very strong life impulse that pushes you to initiate, create, or sometimes teach. In any case, you are noticed, listened to, and followed or imitated.

Caution:

Those who act too long by listening only to their inner momentum often end up alone. To avoid this pitfall, learn how to cultivate emulation rather than competition, cooperation rather than dirigisme.

Social assets that you can easily develop:

- Human warmth and the ability to comfort
- Communicative joy and the ability to make people smile
- Humor, including self-deprecation
- A chivalrous spirit and the ability to protect
- Initiative and the ability to create

Earth dominant (or codominant)

If you have an Earth dominant (or codominant), your best place in society is that of a builder, whether by building, preserving, or consolidating (objects, systems, etc.).

Discreet, observant, calm, and focused, you are a determined person whose best service consists of building or perpetuating things. Often in the background, very moderately interested in power, you need to leave your brand on the world, and you are ready to take your time and mobilize all your forces to this end.

Others know that they can count on you, both for your ability to work and listen, your sense of duty, but also simply for your competence. You will rarely usurp a role that you don't know how to fill, thus contradicting the Peter principle!

Caution:

Be careful not to lock yourself into rigid opinions and inflexible rules, nor to lock others in, not by authoritarianism but by rigor. To avoid this, try to cultivate more emotional and sentimental expressions, desires, and passions . . .

Social assets that you can easily develop:

- Personal strength and the ability to strengthen others
- Clear-headedness and the ability to clarify things
- Self-discipline and the ability to manage systems
- Self-control and the ability to calm situations
- Ambition and the ability to carry out difficult projects

Air dominant (or codominant)

If you have an Air dominant (or a codominant), your best place in society is that of a communicator, whether by informing, pacifying, or gathering.

You naturally flourish in relationships, and you will therefore feel at home in all the roles of meeting others; discussing with them, bringing them together or transmitting information to them.

Sparkling, eternally young-minded, and curious about everything, you are part of the category of people who constitute the social bond of a group; those who make sure people meet, talk, discover each other, and work together.

Diversity seduces you, difference amuses you, and variety feeds you. Resourceful, clever, and often mischievous, you know how to address individuals and crowds, always adopting the most-appropriate behavior and the most-effective words.

Caution:
Your casualness and innate tendency to manipulate won't only make you friends! To avoid this, always be honest and change your mind only after careful consideration.

Social assets that you can easily develop:
- Objectivity and the ability to understand everyone
- Malleability and ability to adapt quickly
- Tolerance and the ability to see the benefits of people or things
- Equity and the ability to judge objectively
- Originality and the ability to bring a new breath of life to things

Water dominant (or codominant)
If you have a Water dominant (or codominant), your best place in society is that of counselor, whether on a medical, spiritual, psychological, or social level.

You almost naturally take on the role of the confidant or the healer, the one with whom we can confide our sufferings; someone who knows how to listen with attention, calm, and depth, because your empathy is great.

You don't like to preach morals, you avoid judging people, and you spontaneously have a culture of secrecy that predisposes you to all roles requiring discretion.

You are dedicated, and very sensitive to environments, atmospheres, and states of soul, and even on the airwaves, your driving force is to understand the invisible, whether it is the soul of people, the meaning of history, the laws of the Universe . . .

Caution:

Be careful that too much receptivity does not end up turning into inertia and weakness, consisting of either giving up or becoming the willing slave of your entourage. To avoid this, know how to set limits, and dare to express your needs and desires in order to thwart unilateral relationships.

Social assets that you can easily develop:

- Psychological subtlety and the ability to love everyone
- Tenderness and the ability to soften people and situations
- Philosophical spirit and the embodiment of spiritual values
- Humanism and the ability to help, relieve, or heal
- Intuition and the ability to transmit faith in life

Astral affinities

We now know that there is no question of rejecting anyone or thinking that a person can be harmful to us just because they are very different. However, to better experience our human relationships, it may also be important to understand how our sensitivity resonates, sometimes dissonantly, with others. This is what we call astral affinities.

Note that the following table is based more on your astrological dominant (as defined in the introduction) than on your sun sign alone. Here's how to read it: look for your dominant in the upper horizontal line and compare it, going down vertically, with all the other dominant ones. The intersecting boxes inform you about the type of relationship you have spontaneously with this or that other zodiacal profile.

	AR	TAU	GEM	CAN	LE	VIR	LI	SCO	SAG	CAP	AQ	PIS
AR	SIM	N	CO	TE	SIM	N	CO+	N	SIM	TE	CO	N
TAU	N	SIM	N	CO	TE	SIM	N	CO+	N	SIM	TE	CO
GEM	CO	N	SIM	N	CO	TE	SIM	N	CO+	N	SIM	TE
CAN	TE	CO	N	SIM	N	CO	TE	SIM	N	CO+	N	SIM
LE	SIM	TE	CO	N	SIM	N	CO	TE	SIM	N	CO+	N
VIR	N	SIM	TE	CO	N	SIM	N	CO	TE	SIM	N	CO+
LI	CO+	N	SIM	TE	CO	N	SIM	N	CO	TE	SIM	N
SCO	N	CO+	N	SIM	TE	CO	N	SIM	N	CO	TE	SIM
SAG	SIM	N	CO+	N	SIM	TE	CO	N	SIM	N	CO	TE
CAP	TE	SIM	N	CO+	N	SIM	TE	CO	N	SIM	N	CO
AQ	CO	TE	SIM	N	CO+	N	SIM	TE	CO	N	SIM	N
PIS	N	CO	TE	SIM	N	CO+	N	SIM	TE	CO	N	SIM

■ **SIM** indicates a similarity relationship: you are very alike, and there are many natural affinities between you; it is a relationship that can refer you back to yourself, including in terms of defects, because they are often shared.

■ **CO** indicates a complementary relationship (CO+ designating the sign with which one possesses the greatest complementarities): although apparently very different, you have a lot to learn from each other, your energies tend to balance each other, and you can maintain a mutually enriching relationship.

■ **TE** indicates a tension relationship: agreement between you isn't always obvious, which does not mean that it is impossible, let alone that it is not mutually enriching. However, each of you works very differently, and it requires respect and tolerance on both sides to make the relationship work.

■ **N** indicates a neutrality relationship: the relationship is a kind of blank sheet at the start (in fact, it depends a lot on other astrological factors) that can evolve into great love, or the most fierce hatred, or even perfect indifference.

NOTE:
It is often mistakenly believed that some signs are more difficult to live with or can be combined, but in reality there is a perfect theoretical equality between the signs, each having three similar signs, three complementary signs (including one more especially), two tension signs, and four neutral signs.

Which people nourish you?

The older I get, the more I find that we can only live with the people who liberate you, who love you with an affection that is as light to wear as it is strong to feel. Life today is too hard, too bitter, too anemic, to be subjected to new servitudes from those we love.

—Albert Camus (dominant: Pluto)

Apart from these astral affinities, we can say that the psychological profile of certain people (men and women combined) reassures you, brightens you up, lets you be totally yourself, allows you to relax; in short, that which does you good.

The type of person who is deeply beneficial to you is indicated in your theme by Jupiter's position as a sign. If you don't know this, you will find, by reading the following, that a specific profile often comes up positively in your life. Once you have identified it (each profile is matched to a certain environment or human group), have the reflex to be in regular contact, because his/her proximity will help you believe in yourself more.

So, if your Jupiter is in:

■ **Aries:** Look for dynamic, reckless, and competitive people. You will find many of them among athletes, especially in extreme sports.

■ **Taurus:** Seek the company of people who are good men, sensual, epicureans, loving the just and the good. You can find them where you find good food (in a cooking class or at your local delicatessen store, for example).

■ **Gemini:** Look for people who are fun, curious, and sociable. You will find many of them in education and in cultural centers.

■ **Cancer:** Seek the company of gentle people, loving children, interested in the imaginary. You will find many in family spaces (parks, gardens, schools).

■ **Leo:** Look for charismatic, creative people with strong personalities and at least one passion. Many of them can be found in theater classes and cultural venues.

■ **Virgo:** Seek the company of reasonable, helpful people, capable of moderation and solidarity. There are many of them in modest communities and in the public service.

■ **Libra:** Look for people who are conciliatory and peaceful, with a strong sense of harmony and aesthetics. Many of them can be found in exhibition spaces, diplomatic organizations, and art workshops.

■ **Scorpio:** Seek the company of people interested in the transformation of things or, more generally, in all matters relating to the human soul. You will find a lot of them in social structures, the world of personal development, and psychology.

■ **Sagittarius:** Look for dynamic, optimistic, and open-minded people. They love travel and all the structures related to tourism.

■ **Capricorn:** Look for the company of people interested in major social causes, all those concerned with issues of human organization. You will find them mainly in political and activist structures, as well as among intellectuals, all horizons combined.

■ **Aquarius:** Look for the presence of friendly people, interested in avant-garde ideas and eager to act as a group. You will find them in large numbers in humanist associations and foundations.

■ **Pisces:** Look for the company of those who are interested in human psychology and transcendence in all its forms. They often frequent religious and artistic structures.

ILLUSIONS AND PATHOLOGIES OF THE SELF

The greatest discovery of all time is that human beings can change their lives by changing their mental attitudes.

—Albert Schweitzer (dominant: Uranus)

Everyone is unique

To put it bluntly, one could say that, like everything else, a human being's life can go wrong. There is therefore a healthy functioning (which predisposes happiness and makes others happy) and a functioning that can be described as pathological or, at the very least, toxic, which predisposes misery and creates misfortune all round.

Any meaningful personal-development technique must help the individual identify and then achieve his or her most healthful mode of functioning. By remaining faithful to his natural inclination, he will be able to preserve his serenity, especially during difficult moments, because he will have confidence in himself and will know that what happens to him not only makes sense but is also necessary for his evolution.

We must therefore understand that each of us sees, hears, feels, perceives, and conceives the world according to his own basic mental filters. We do not have the same perception of things, and that is very good (since, as we have seen in the previous pages, this is the wealth of humanity).

Mental filters

To understand how each person is unique and to respect this singularity, it is essential to identify our mental filters and then to observe whether our personal reading grid is working well. We must, in a way, take a personal look at the situation and ask ourselves this question: "Where am I at with myself?"

In astrology, every factor has a downside and an upside, a dark side and a bright side. This vision is full of hope because, if you work on yourself, you can turn any disability into an asset, any weakness into strength. It is not a figure of speech; it is a reality that everyone can experience!

So we will now see what, on the positive side, is your main driving force and what, on the negative side, is your main poison; that is, the lie you can very naturally tell yourself, the illusion into which you can most easily fall and that will stop your personal evolution by locking you in toxic mode.

Good news!
By developing a healthful state, a behavior pattern in harmony with your deep nature and thus emphasizing your qualities and assets, the unhealthful state will disappear on its own.

What illusion is poisoning you?

The mind is its own place and in itself, can make a Heaven of Hell, a Hell of Heaven.

—John Milton (dominant: Neptune)

According to your zodiacal dominant, here are the toxic mental states that predominate in youand how to remedy them by developing corresponding healthful mental states.

53

WHO AM I?

Aries

Your root illusion could be summed up as "I can be happy by myself." There is frequent confusion between, on the one hand, your predisposition to autonomy and independence and, on the other, a mistaken belief that you can achieve happiness independently, despite your surroundings, or even against them! This is actually impossible—your happiness will never be complete or lasting if you make the mistake of building it in a self-centered frame of mind.

Cultivating love is the best remedy for you.

Taurus

Your root illusion could be summed up as thinking that happiness is something that is obtained and maintained. There is frequent confusion between your predisposition to assimilate things and use them to build other things (materially, intellectually, and even emotionally) and a mistaken belief that you can achieve happiness by simply accumulating the sources of well-being forever! In reality this is impossible, because we always end up losing the goods and people we care for most. Your happiness will never be complete or lasting if you make the mistake of building it too greedily.

Cultivating detachment is the best remedy for you.

Gemini

Your root illusion could be summed up as thinking that nothing is safe and that everything is relative and changing. There is frequent confusion between your predisposition to learn and understand multiple points of view and a mistaken belief that you can achieve happiness by changing your behavior and direction with the wind.

This is actually impossible, because if you don't have a solid compass that shows you a general direction to stay true to, you always end up getting lost. Your happiness will never be complete or lasting if you make the mistake of building it with a too-elastic vision of life.

Cultivating commitment (ideological, emotional, professional) is the best remedy for you.

Cancer

Your root illusion could be summed up as thinking that happiness is something intimate that has nothing to do with the rest of the world. There is frequent confusion between, on the one hand, your predisposition to provide and receive warmth and tenderness from your own people and, on the other hand, a mistaken belief that you can achieve happiness by withdrawing into your intimate sphere. This is actually impossible, because social life always ends up affecting privacy, and you cannot live in total autarky. Your happiness will never be complete or lasting if you make the mistake of building it too intimately.

Cultivating ambition and socio-professional objectives is the best remedy for you.

Leo

Your root illusion could be summed up as "the world revolves around me." There is frequent confusion in you between your predisposition to shine, guide, and be heard and a mistaken belief that you can achieve happiness without regard for the rest of your community, or by simply leading it without listening to its components. In reality this is impossible ,because, however talented one may be, one is poor if one does not share one's strengths with those around you. Your happiness will never be complete or lasting if you make the mistake of building it without consideration for others.

Cultivating cooperation and friendships is the best remedy for you.

Virgo

Your root illusion could be summed up by thinking that everything that is really important can be analyzed and understood, because there is frequent confusion between your predisposition to reason and to dissect in detail and a mistaken belief that you can achieve happiness by ignoring everything that is invisible in this world (whether it is the unconscious, feelings, or esoteric laws). This is in fact impossible because, however serious and voluntary you may be, you will remain deprived of a part of yourself if you attach too much importance only to visible, measurable, and purely rational things. Your happiness will never be complete or lasting if you make the mistake of building it too narrowly by reducing your objectives to utilitarian and "sensible."

Cultivating a strong spirituality as well as a strong sentimentality is the best remedy for you.

Libra

Your root illusion could be summed up as thinking that nothing is of value unless it's shared. There is frequent confusion between your predisposition to love, cooperate, and function well as a couple or in association and a mistaken belief that happiness is possible only for two people. As long as you base your development on external conditions, or on one or more other people, you will experience an emotional dependence that is incompatible with your true happiness. It will never be complete or durable if you make the mistake of thinking of it as necessarily depending on your human relationships.

Cultivating a strong autonomy as well as a strong individuality is the best remedy for you.

Scorpio

Your root illusion could be summed up as thinking that since nothing is permanent, then nothing is of value or importance, because there is frequent confusion between your predisposition to perceive and adapt to the many changes required by life and a mistaken belief that true happiness does not exist, that everything is relative or temporary.

As long as you base your thinking on a form of cynicism or immediate enjoyment (such as quickly taking advantage of something before it disappears), you will experience inner instability that is incompatible with your growth. It will never be complete or sustainable until you fully understand that, of course, everything ends but that each end is also followed by a new beginning. Therefore, a notion of eternity exists.

Cultivating philosophy or spirituality (start with all questions and answers about death) as well as a moderation in immediate enjoyment is the best remedy for you.

Sagittarius
Your root illusion could be summed up as "I know what I'm talking about and so I'm right." There is frequent confusion between your predisposition to understand the world with a broad-minded synthesis, your pedagogical skills in explaining things to others, and a mistaken belief that there is a worldview (which you wrongly call true) superior to others. As long as you keep your thoughts about a form of dogmatism and you continue trying to convince rather than explain, you will experience many conflicts and frustrations that will prevent you from enjoying serene happiness. It will never be complete or sustainable until you have fully understood that while it is important to have convictions, there is only one step between certainty and fanaticism or intolerance.

Cultivating a plurality of approaches and thoughts (and socializing with people of all persuasions and beliefs) is the best remedy for you.

Capricorn
Your root illusion could be summed up as thinking that individual happiness is possible only in a generally happy society, because there is frequent confusion between your predisposition to think on a large scale (with an interest in at least one area of public life: intellectual, political, economic, industrial, artistic, etc.) and the mistaken belief that it is futile to seek happiness in a society that functions poorly.

As long as you base your thinking on the certainty that favorable social conditions are the only guarantee of well-being, you will never be satisfied. You can be so only if you understand that while it is important to act in a collective perspective but that there is no perfect model outside the one called Utopia, happiness is variable according to people.

Cultivating intimate joys (love, family to start with) is the best remedy for you.

Aquarius

Your root illusion could be summed up by thinking that individual happiness is simply another name for friendship, because there is frequent confusion in you between your predisposition to fraternize, cooperate, and feel comfortable in a group and a mistaken belief that it is in the community that you can find your serenity. As long as you make your happiness by relying on others (including by trying to remake the world with them), you will never be satisfied. You can be so only by understanding that while it is important to have friends and common projects, if everyone makes the mistake of losing his own identity, then no one will be happy.

Cultivating personal activities and giving equal importance to love as to brotherhood is the best remedy for you.

Pisces

Your root illusion could be summed up as thinking that only invisible laws are ultimately important, because there is frequent confusion in you between your predisposition to capture wavelengths, to feel moods and people, and to have dazzling intuitions and a mistaken belief that the life of the mind and soul is enough to be happy. As long as you base your happiness on an "elsewhere" (and at the same time flee the real world), you will never be satisfied. You can be so only if you understand that while it is important to cultivate a rich spirituality, it makes sense only if it is applied in everyday life, if it serves the concrete.

Multiplying down-to-earth activities while giving importance to matter and body (at least as much as to the soul) is the best remedy for you.

What is your primary dissatisfaction (frustration)?

In addition to a particular type of illusion, each of us has a particular type of frustration, a kind of innate dissatisfaction concerning an area of life. Identifying it is the first step to progression.

To identify your primary dissatisfaction, turn to your dominant elemental.

Fire dominant (or codominant)

Your primary dissatisfaction concerns your personal growth, which may never seem big enough or important enough for you. You always want to become something more (taller, smarter . . .), to improve yourself, to stand out from the crowd, but because of this, you can be very hard on yourself (and on those around you). The saying "The best is the enemy of the good" suits you perfectly.

Rather than thinking about the next battle to be fought, celebrate the one you just won. Rather than thinking about the next project to launch, take the time to refine the current one. Rather than always demanding more from yourself and others, rejoice in what everyone already does.

It is not a question of curbing your wings, nor of turning away from the summits, but rather of making you feel better in the present, of stopping yourself from feeling guilty (and making others feel guilty). Start by repeating this to yourself: "If I do my best, then I have no further judgment to pass on the result."

Earth dominant (or codominant)

Your primary dissatisfaction concerns your material growth, which may never seem big enough or important enough for you.

You always want to possess more, to get richer (on all levels), and because of this, you can be very hard on yourself (and on those around you). The saying "Biting off more than one can chew" suits you perfectly.

Rather than thinking about the next purchase, take advantage of the one you just made. Rather than thinking about the next degree you want to obtain, use the one you have already obtained. Rather than always demanding more from life, enjoy what you already have.

It is not a question of cutting off your funds, but rather of making you feel better in the present, of stopping yourself from ruminating about all that remains to be done without seeing what you have already achieved. Start by repeating this to yourself: "What I am is not what I own."

Air dominant (or codominant)

Your primary dissatisfaction concerns your intellectual growth, which may never seem big enough or important enough for you. You always want to know more—to know more people, places, and things—and because of this, you can be very hard on yourself (and on those around you). The saying "All talk and no action" suits you perfectly.

Rather than pondering and theorizing, do something concrete. Rather than thinking, imagining, and planning, use your knowledge to put things in place. Rather than always wanting to discover more about life, use what you already know to see where it leads you.

It is not a question of cutting you off from the world, but rather of making you feel better in the present, of stopping yourself being a spectator in life and becoming an actor in it. Start by repeating this to yourself: "What I am is not what I know."

Water dominant (or codominant)

Your primary dissatisfaction concerns your emotional growth, which may never seem big enough or important enough for you.

You always want to feel more, to love more, to know more about osmosis, and because of this, you can be very hard on yourself (and on those around you). The saying "The heart has its reasons, of which reason knows nothing" suits you perfectly.

Rather than being constantly heckled by your emotions and feelings, clarify situations. Instead of "taking the heat" without protesting, learn to express your feelings better. Rather than always wanting more attention, show compassion without expecting anything in return.

It's not about cutting you off from your heart but rather of making yourself feel better in the present and stopping from being tossed around by your emotions. Start by repeating this to yourself: "What I am doesn't depend on who loves me."

What is your inner poison?

Finally, astrology can also help us fight against our fundamental negative tendency, which is often the root of all our other defects and can be defined as a kind of inner poison that pollutes and weakens us.

Here again, we will use the dominant of your theme, as defined in the introduction.

Fire dominant (or codominant)

Your main poison is aversion.
You tend to reject violently and want to destroy, more or less consciously, everything you don't like. Easily dissatisfied, critical, and quarrelsome, you feel contempt and anger for everything that is beyond your control or not as you would like.

Therefore, there is strength but also rigidity in you.

Earth dominant (or codominant)

Your main poison is greed.
You tend to want more and more, never to be satisfied. There is a predisposition to addiction, a weakness in the face of pleasure and the senses that obscures your judgment and all too often lets your primary instincts speak for themselves. You are insatiable, often obstinate, and jealous, and the risks of dependence are very high.

There is a strong but also a great need for you to take ownership of things and people.

ADVICE:
Once our illusions, frustrations, deficiencies, and poisons have been identified, it is a matter of not identifying with them: we are not our defects. The problems of our personalities are only transient and are possible to overcome.

Air dominant (or codominant)

Your main poison is doubt.

You tend to want to understand and explain everything and systematically look for reasons and justifications for everything. However, one idea sweeps away the other, and all this causes instability in you, no longer knowing to which saint you should dedicate yourself, which thought to follow, which solution to favor.

There is a lot of finesse in you, but also, without commitment or faith, a tendency to lose yourself and become paralyzed by hesitation.

Water dominant (or codominant)

Your main poison is illusion.

You tend to follow your emotions, and since they constantly change, you often feel confused, evolving in a chaotic life, pulled in many directions by circumstances and people. You are passive and easily upset, and your inner world is complex as well as perplexing.

There is a great depth of soul in you, but also disorder and emotional agitation.

Your basic deficiency, becoming resilient with Saturn

Astrology teaches us one important thing: each of us, as lucky as he seems to have been at birth, begins his life with a deficiency, a void that he will have to "fill" by himself over time.

This basic deficiency is, in our individual themes, indicated by Saturn's position (first as a sign, then as a sector, and sometimes as an aspect, but it becomes secondary).

If you know your theme, you need only to refer to the following to identify your initial lack and understand how to fill it, understanding that it is an integral part of your personal evolutionary path.

ADVICE

If you don't know Saturn's place, you can try to guess it by reading the following or, of course, by having your theme realized by a professional practitioner. This help can be invaluable in setting up a number of solutions and systems to fill the saturnine gap.

In any case, it is important to keep in mind that the essence of life is benevolence and that this basic deficiency is not a gratuitous punishment or deprivation: on the contrary, by becoming resilient (i.e., by strengthening yourself internally in the face adversity), you also become more capable of building authentic happiness, on the basis of your ability to cope.

If your Saturn is in Aries

There is a lack of self-assertion and initiative, shyness, and relational clumsiness. Your will is difficult to express, and your personality has often been built in a more defensive than offensive way, more passive than active.

EXAMPLE

With her Saturn in Aries, Virginia never knew her father and was raised by a woman overwhelmed by her situation as a single mother, not very resourceful and not daring to shout, oppose, or impose herself. Virginia has never learned to say no or stop, let alone express what she wants. However, it will be important for her to be able to reinsert the strength of her desires into her will, thus reconciling herself with her deep motivations rather than continuing to live as she is told to live and without making too much noise.

If your Saturn is in Taurus

You have lacked security and stability, which has resulted in a compulsive need to accumulate or own and yet be unable to fully enjoy it or be reassured by your environment. You have an irrational fear of losing your belongings and your friends.

If your Saturn is in Gemini

You have suffered from a lack of communication that has led to a lack of or difficult sociability, sometimes resulting in suboptimal development of your expression, language, and thinking skills. You lack confidence in your ideas and intelligence and express the need to hold on to proven information (which locks you into preconceived ideas).

If your Saturn is in Cancer

You are in need of a family; your childhood may have been sad, cold ,and full of limitations or prohibitions. You suffer (or have suffered) from a feeling of isolation or abandonment, with an austere or restricted family home, sometimes very modest in material terms. Some major emotional problems with the family may have affected you, such as rejection or the absence of a parent.

If your Saturn is in Leo

You have lacked recognition and love, which has made it difficult to love yourself, to respect yourself, to experience dignity, and to identify yourself. A feeling of imperfection or insignificance leads to dissatisfaction and self-deprecation. You're afraid you don't deserve the affection of others.

If your Saturn is in Virgo

You have lacked social integration (this is sometimes due to poor health or a family environment that, in one way or another, has been on the margins of the rest of society). The result is a sense of uselessness and incapacity that you lack today. Often, mental conditioning causes one to imprison oneself in principles, prohibitions, and taboos. This may be the case for you.

If your Saturn is in Libra

It is likely that there was a lack of harmony and support during your youth. Under these conditions, it is very difficult to find peace in your human relationships, because you have not learned how to reconcile, understand, or listen. The result is a difficulty in collaborating and an inner conflict between your need for love and your refusal to reach the necessary consensus.

If your Saturn is in Scorpio

You lacked privacy and respect for your instincts. You have had an education probably based on the forbidden, the shame of the body, or a total disregard for the notions of intimacy and personal space. This leads to a feeling that the impulses are dangerous or scandalous, which prevents you from achieving harmony between the unconscious and the conscious.

If your Saturn is in Sagittarius

A lack of faith, optimism, and a positive vision of life have made you feel that life today is absurd. The prevailing impressions are disorientation and uncertainty; you often lack the landmarks, principles, and beliefs to which you can cling (your parents did not believe in anything or had ideas so different from yours that you could not adopt them).

If your Saturn is in Capricorn

You lacked ambition and responsibility (i.e., you suffered from disempowerment). As a result, you are desperately looking for social recognition. Often, you have a feeling of failure, of being "good for nothing" (perhaps because you were told too often when you were a child). You have the feeling that you are unable to succeed, that you are unable to do anything important.

If your Saturn is in Aquarius

You suffer from a lack of sociability and have the feeling that you do not belong to any community and that you are not part of a larger whole. A shy and introverted childhood has led you to feel that you cannot be accepted by others as you are, because you are very (too) different, and that your uniqueness, in one way or another, is a problem.

If your Saturn is in Pisces

A lack of protection or sensitivity in your surroundings, or even, more rarely, the general impression of not having any luck and being the victim of far too many ordeals, leads you to feel overwhelmed by life or, at the very least, makes you suspicious of your fate and others. As a result, you tend to withdraw into yourself in a defensive manner.

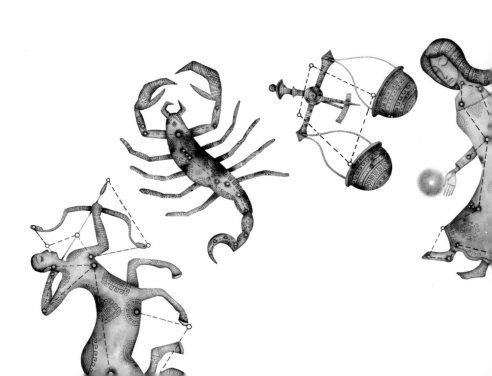

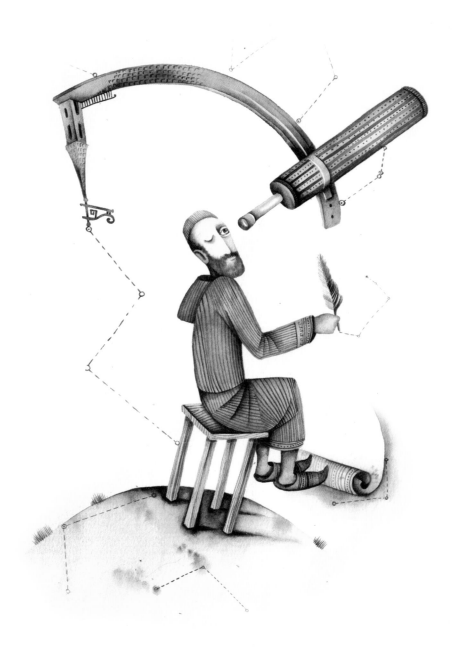

WORKING ON
YOURSELF

KNOWING HOW TO USE YOUR POTENTIAL

Achieving a perfect realization of its nature is why we are all here.

—Oscar Wilde (dominant: Saturn)

Twelve signs, twelve fundamental researches

We have just seen that astrology is able to give us valuable information about the main illusions and frustrations that we may encounter, depending on our theme. However, we can, and must, see the dynamic engines that animate our sky, because these energies represent powerful fuel in our lives and can make us smile and give us vitality, if we take the trouble to cultivate them.

Let's now look at the positive impulses that predominate, again according to your zodiacal dominant. To better understand the archetype specific to each sign, we have systematically associated an adjective with it in order to better understand its deep essence. Above all, it is this quality of sign that that you must allow to be freely expressed at home to feel good and have all the energy you need to cope.

Aries: instinctive
An imperative: to be

Your engine is a powerful life impulse, a constant desire to feel alive. This pushes you to stay active, to be willing to start new things and take on new challenges.

Do not cut yourself off from your impulses, your desires, and your instincts. Learn how to control them so that you do not become their slave, but without suffocating them.

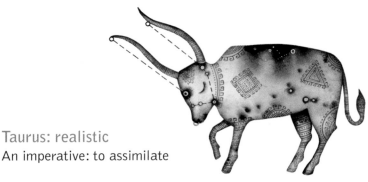

Taurus: realistic
An imperative: to assimilate

Your motor is a powerful desire to assimilate experiences and knowledge in order to expand your life, to fill it. This pushes you to be both hardworking and greedy, alternating periods when you seek external materials to feed yourself (in the form of affection, training, material goods, etc.) and those when you enjoy them quietly, when you enjoy the fruits of your efforts.

Do not cut yourself off from this acquisition/joy process, but learn not to become its slave by falling into insatiable greed.

Gemini: sociable
An imperative: to know

Your engine is a powerful desire to discover and learn. This pushes you to be sociable and mobile, to be interested in all the ways to obtain and transmit information (dialogue, writing, video, etc.).

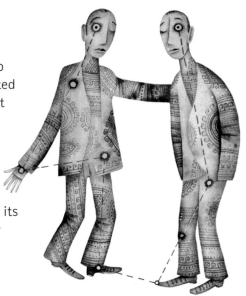

Do not cut yourself off from this intense curiosity that is your inner spring, but be careful not to become its victim by falling into intellectual (or professional) dispersion and superficiality in your human relationships.

Cancer: emotional
An imperative: to feel

Your motor is a powerful desire to share your emotions and cherish your loved ones. This pushes you to be connected to yourself, tender and intimate, to be more concerned than others about your family, your home, but also your inner world.

Don't cut yourself off from the intense emotionality that is your reason for existing. On the other hand, it is a question of not becoming a slave to it by falling into hypersensitivity or vagrancy in your imagination.

Leo: sentimental
An imperative: to create

Your driving force is a powerful desire to give an external shape to what you feel in your heart, whether it is sentimentally through love relationships, family wise through parenthood, or creatively through your artistic or intellectual works.

Do not cut yourself off from this intense need to "share your heart," which is your inner compass, but do not become its slave by sinking into devastating passions.

Virgo: cerebral
An imperative: to understand

Your engine is a powerful desire to understand the world and people. This pushes you to develop your analytical and critical faculties, to show reason and logic, to attach yourself to details without leaving anything out.

Do not cut yourself off from this intense need to dissect things—this is what carries and guides you—but do not be a slave to it by falling into obsessions or a narrowness of view.

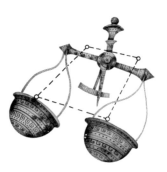

Libra: cooperative
An imperative: to love

Your engine is a powerful desire to be in a couple and to "work" with others (intimately as well as professionally), because you need this external view to feel complete. This pushes you to cultivate diplomacy, savoir vivre, and impartiality.

Do not cut yourself off from this intense need to love and be loved—it is your reason for living—but be careful not to fall into dependence on others.

Scorpio: driven
An imperative: to live intensely

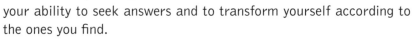

Your driving force is a powerful desire to live intensely and to the end of each situation, even painful ones, because you feel that everything life offers is a lesson. This pushes you to cultivate your ability to seek answers and to transform yourself according to the ones you find.

Do not cut yourself off from this intense need to experiment and evolve, but beware of falling into extremes (sensual passions, dangerous activities, borderline behaviors, etc.).

Sagittarius: idealistic
An imperative: to give meaning to life

Your engine is a powerful desire for meaning, because you claim that nothing happens by chance and that life, however complex it may be, must have a hidden meaning. This leads you to take an interest in everything related to humanity but also, often, in symbolism, philosophy, and any thought aimed at synthesizing the world.

Do not cut yourself off from this intense quest for meaning, but be careful not to fall into a single, dogmatic, even fanatical truth.

Capricorn: pragmatic
An imperative: to leave your mark

Your engine is a powerful desire to make a significant contribution to the world. This pushes you to take an interest, to cultivate ambitious goals, and to make an enormous effort to achieve them by becoming more educated, more competent, and more influential every day.

Do not cut yourself off from this intense need to do important things in your life. Avoid, however, the trap of pursuing an inaccessible goal that prevents you from being satisfied with the present.

Aquarius: progressive
An imperative: to renew

Your engine is a powerful desire to know what tomorrow will bring and then to carry this innovation as quickly as possible into the present. This pushes you to be interested in everything that is modern, avant-garde, and original but also to associate with all kinds of original people and to cooperate with them.

Do not cut yourself off from this intense need to participate in groups that want to "remake the world," but do not become slaves by feeling obliged to impose your views and by constantly living in a supposedly better but hypothetical future.

Pisces: intuitive
An imperative: to transcend

Your driving force is a powerful desire to connect to something greater than humankind, whether through faith, creative inspiration, or meditative communion with nature and the universe. This pushes you to cultivate a very rich spirituality and inner life, to live with your "feelers out," and to develop qualities of soul such as empathy and compassion.

Do not cut yourself off from this intense need to elevate your being above matter, but do not break with reality by sinking into superstition, bigotry, fanaticism, enlightenment, or, simply, a totally distorted vision of reality.

From the individual to the universal

Life calls, not for perfection, but for completeness.

—Carl Gustave Jung (dominant: Mars)

Each of us has our own personal tendencies, and not to follow them would condemn us to painful conformity. However, it doesn't mean that we should believe that we are all irremediably different and therefore alone in ourselves. In this respect, astrology delivers a strong message: everyone is unique but we are all the same! Although we all have unique fingerprints, we are all human beings with the same members and organs; therefore each of us must be seen in the light of our particularities and be able to identity ourselves in others: we are both unique and, at the same time, alike. Human beings from all times and places not only are made of the same biological materials but also have the same needs and aspirations: not to suffer physically, to love, to be able to express themselves, etc.

NOTE:
Astrology teaches us that any human being needs to nourish twelve distinct functions.

In an astrological theme, everything is about proportions. The ingredients are the same for everyone (the Sun, the Moon, the ascendant, the twelve signs, the twelve sectors, etc.), but their distribution and their combinations differ for each person.

All human beings have the same needs to be happy.
Certainly their priorities are changing, but in the end, each part of them must be nourished so that they can be at peace. These parts are represented by the astrological factors found in any sky chart.

Human beings are made up of universal (cosmic) elements, which, by embodying themselves in a particular place and time, become individual.

It is therefore illusory to believe that one is a being apart, isolated, separated, and fundamentally different, or that it is impossible to really understand the other because this other person cannot feel the same things or experience the same needs.

Astrology helps us understand that all humans (and even all forms of life) need to nourish functions that can be described as universal. It is simply human nature, and the importance we attach to them differs from one individual to another.

Being able to identify these functions renders a double service to anyone seeking advancement in life. Not only does this make it possible to understand how others really resemble us deeply (which promotes tolerance and a sense of belonging to a human family and an open heart and a sense of security), but also, in a more introspective way, to reflect on how, personally, each person nourishes universal functions.

NOTE:
It is interesting to ask ourselves how, individually, we respond to these needs, because perhaps we will find that we have left out this or that essential need (and sometimes for a very long time!).

Twelve basic and universal needs

Reading these twelve basic needs, you will notice how the obstruction of any of them immediately plunges society into a type of dictatorship, which prohibits, for example, freedom of thought (Mercury) or freedom of expression (Sun), assembly (Uranus), or religion (Neptune). In this sense, not only does astrology define the fundamental needs of the human being, but, consequently, it also describes fundamental freedoms that must be present in any human society seeking the happiness of its citizens.

■ **The Sun** makes every human being need to assert his or her personality freely, without being prevented, offended, punished, or humiliated. Is this your case?

■ **The Moon** makes every human being need to feel safe, in a safe environment and among people with whom to build trust and tenderness. Is this your case?

■ **Mercury** makes every human being need to be able to move where he wants and meet whomever he chooses. Is this your case?

■ **Venus** makes every human being need to be able to cultivate values that are specific to him, to love whom he desires, and to surround himself with what seems beautiful to him. Is this your case?

■ **Mars** makes every human being need to be able to act without hindrance, to be active, to be enterprising, and to enjoy his own body as he sees fit. Is this your case?

■ **Ceres** makes every human being need to be able to integrate a group of fellow humans, to find his place, to feel useful, and to defend the ethics that he considers right. Is this your case?

■ **Jupiter** makes every human being need to be able to travel, to get to know other cultures, and to develop a personal philosophy of life. Is this your case?

■ **Saturn** makes every human being need to be able to participate in the organization and decision-making of the society to which he belongs, on a small or large scale; that is, at least in his family. Is this your case?

■ **Uranus** makes every human being need to be able to surround himself with friends with whom he shares a common vision of the world or common projects, and to be able to interact freely and in synergy with them. Is this your case?

■ **Neptune** makes every human being need to be able to cultivate his spirituality, develop his faith in a secular or religious system, and connect with a community that shares this belief, this ideal. Is this your case?

■ **Pluto** makes every human being need to be able to freely start a new life; that is, move away from his or her usual environment (divorce, for example), or change work (reorientation), change religion (conversion). Is this your case?

■ Finally, **the Black Moon** makes every human being need to be able to criticize freely, without reprisals, the opinions of others, to doubt everything that is proposed to him, and to express a right of reserve in the face of everything that does not suit him. Is this your case?

IMPORTANT
Freedom of power does not mean duty. For example, if you are not interested in the organization of public life, being able to take decisions concerning the community (Saturn) is a possibility that guarantees you to live in a democracy, but it is by no means an obligation.

Sectors, typical schedule

At the same time, it is wise to balance our timetable carefully to allow us time to cultivate each domain in our lives, because this is one of the messages contained in the very structure of the astrological theme: the division of the theme into twelve sectors (also called houses) tells us that human life should give importance to each of the domains represented by these sectors.

As before with the planets, the distribution and importance of the sectors are different from one person to another, and the astrologer, in a personalized approach, will be able to help everyone establish their priorities.

However, we can already reflect here, more generally, on how we invest our time. For example, are there any areas that are overrepresented or, on the contrary, underrepresented in our time schedule? Can't we try to put more balance into all this?

Thus, ideally, part of the day (or, at worst, the week) should be allocated to each of the following areas, because, in the light of the universe and cosmic law, each one is essential to the proper functioning of the individual: to neglect one is to automatically create an imbalance.

> **NOTE:**
> Every person's birth chart is divided into twelve sectors; each sector represents a field of life to which—more or less according to their individual theme—time, importance, and energy should be given. Long-term neglect of one or more of these sectors would be tantamount to sealing off any room for development.

Sector I
Invites us to spend time and energy on our body and appearance.

Ask yourself: *Have I taken care of my body today, or have I neglected this aspect of my life?*

Why should I do it? Because it allows us to respect others and ourselves by presenting the best of ourselves.

Sector II
Invites us to spend time and energy on increasing our knowledge, our experience, and our inner and outer wealth.

Ask yourself: *Have I gained something today, am I somehow richer than yesterday, or have I neglected this aspect of my life?*

Why should I do it? Because it allows us to gain more knowledge, wisdom, and wealth.

Sector III
Invites us to spend time and energy on taking walks, taking part in discussions, reading, getting up-to-date information, discovering, learning.

Ask yourself: *Have I understood/discovered something or someone today, or have I neglected this aspect of my life?*

Why should I do it? Because it allows us to stay young in mind and to renew our thinking and outlook on life.

Sector IV
Invites us to spend time and energy on enjoying our loved ones, having intimate moments, and taking the time to rest, relax, and dream.

Ask yourself: *Have I had a quiet moment today (alone or with a loved one), or have I neglected this aspect of my life?*

Why should I do it? Because it allows us to feel part of something larger than ourselves and to relax.

Sector V
Invites us to spend time and energy on generating one thing or another, to bring out emotions and feelings through our creations but also through our loves, including the love for our children.

Ask yourself: *Have I taken a moment today to express what I feel or to be creative (or both), or have I neglected this aspect of my life?*

Why should I do it? Because it allows us to stay connected to our intimate truth, our vital power.

Sector VI
Invites us to spend time and energy on contributing to society, to others, to the world. This can simply involve work or any profitable activity beyond oneself.

Ask yourself: *Have I done something useful today, something profitable for at least someone other than myself, or have I neglected this aspect of my life?*

Why should I do it? Because it allows us to feel integrated, to find our place, and to contribute to the smooth running of the social network to which we belong.

Sector VII
Invites us to spend time and energy on cultivating close relationships (work or affection) with other individuals, to learn to live and do things together.

Ask yourself: *Have I done something with someone today, or have I neglected this aspect of my life?*

Why should I do it? Because it allows us to avoid sinking into individualism, a vision that is too monolithic.

Sector VIII

Invites us to spend time and energy on fulfilling our instincts and desires, starting with sexuality. More subtly, this sector asks us not to forget sharing, not of superficial things (such as leisure or sexuality reduced to its sole dimension of pleasure) but of emotions, sensations, ideas, projects, energies . . .

Ask yourself: *Have I shared anything important today, or have I neglected this aspect of my life?*

Why should I do it? Because it keeps us from sinking into frustration and selfishness.

Sector IX

Invites us to spend time and energy on discovering new and reflective things (not just having fun, but to really discover something new). This can involve travel, conferences or debates, readings, studies . . .

Ask yourself: *Have I learned something important today or had an informative and enriching discussion, or have I neglected this aspect of my life?*

Why should I do it? Because it allows us to broaden our vision of life.

Sector X

Invites us to spend time and energy on achieving important objectives, requiring effort and perseverance. This may concern our career but also more-personal goals and nonprofessional ambitions.

Ask yourself: *Have I pursued a long-term task today, or have I neglected this aspect of my life?*

Why should I do it? Because it allows us to give something of ourselves its place in history and to structure our lives.

Sector XI

Invites us to spend time and energy on cultivating our friendships and developing activities and projects in our community to try to build a better world.

Ask yourself: *Have I spoken to people with whom I have common goals and participated in something collective today, or have I neglected this aspect of my life?*

Why should I do it? Because it allows us to be part of a collective synergy that can change the course of things on a social scale.

Sector XII

Invites us to spend time and energy on reflection, meditation, and spiritual practices.

Ask yourself: *Have I taken the time today to connect to my deep self or the universe (or both)?*

Why should I do it? Because it allows us to find unexpected resources within ourselves.

Paying attention to oneself and the world

Attention is not only about vigilance. To be attentive to oneself and others is to accept and respect oneself, to accept and respect others.

This can change everything, including situations that seem intractable. It should be noted that acceptance has nothing to do with passivity. It opposes rejection. Acceptance is the integration of everything that we are (or everything that the other is), and is only the beginning of a process that leads us to evolve.

It is essential to start by recognizing all that is within us in order to have a chance to work on it afterward. Here again, astrology is a very valuable tool since it is the only objective means at our disposal to determine exactly our potential and to question us about its realization.

The astral theme "lays out" what is to be to ensure we pay attention to it and that we accept it. Once you have done it for yourself, it becomes easy to do it for your loved ones, then for your acquaintances, and finally for the whole world. Astrology, by offering us an interpretation of the human soul, allows us to see that there is no theme (and therefore no one) without dissonance (darkness, defects) or, conversely, without assonance (light, qualities).

Once it's accepted for yourself, you can identify what is going well, what is not going well, and what could be improved. Everyone can balance their strengths and weaknesses to work to bring out the best in themselves.

Be careful, yes, but of what?

The attention that we pay to ourselves and to others can be subdivided into four fields, or elements:

■ **The body,** which, in astrology, refers us to the Earth element, the heaviest and most material of the elements

■ **Feelings,** which are related to the Fire element, the most intense but also the most fleeting of the elements

■ **The spirit,** which is astrologically related to the Air element, the most invisible, the most subtle of the elements

■ **The soul,** which is astrologically related to Water, the most transformable element (e.g., fog, steam, moving water, ice) and the most essential to life

Depending on your dominant elemental (see p. 11), you can focus your attention on one of the following four fields.

If your dominant is Earth

It is important, in case of difficulty or suffering, to focus your attention first on what is happening in your body. Can you locate where and how pain (including whether it is psychic and emotional) manifests itself in your flesh? Does your throat tighten, does your stomach burn, does your jaw tighten, do you feel a fever or, on the contrary, chills? Any palpitations or itching? And so on.

Then ask yourself: *Am I just that part of my body?* The answer is no.

If your dominant is Fire

It is important, in case of difficulty or suffering, to focus your attention first on your dominant feelings and moods. Do you feel sad, angry, alone, jealous, lost, scared, desperate, lacking something?

Then accept this feeling, even if you can decide to turn it into something positive; welcome it like an injured animal that you are going to heal.

Then ask yourself: *Am I just that feeling?* The answer is no.

If your dominant is Air

It is important, in case of difficulty or suffering, to focus your attention first on your thoughts, on the images that are formed in your mind, the judgments and often-frozen points of view that result from them. What reasons do you give to justify your misfortune or suffering? Is your thinking really personal and relevant to the situation, or are you simply repeating what your education has taught you, or words already spoken in past situations that you find similar to the present?

Then ask yourself: *Am I just that thought?* The answer is no.

If your dominant is Water

It is important, in case of difficulty or suffering, to focus your attention first on your soul; that is, on the part of life and light that, in all circumstances (even the darkest), continues to shine, even weakly. There is always wisdom in us, but we must let it be expressed. If you were a great sage, how would you react now? It's time to calm down and meditate on all this.

Then ask yourself: *Am I just this pain?* The answer is no.

> **NOTE:**
> In any case, it is a question of accepting what is and then making it evolve; that is, accepting reality but without identifying one's being or life (and freezing them) in a situation that is necessarily temporary. In other words, it is important not to confuse what you are experiencing at a given moment with what you are in depth.

Somatization and messages sent by your body

Our theme contains the four elements previously listed because we are all made up of a body, a soul, feelings, and thoughts. If everyone can approach the question of attention from one angle rather than another (someone who focuses on the body will do yoga, for example), it is a matter of starting a process that focuses on each of the four dimensions of being, one after the other.

So, whatever your astrological type, attention to the body will give you the leads to understand your unconscious patterns, the things you are trying to hide from yourself.

What is known as "the zodiac man" is a traditional astrological pattern that establishes correspondences between each sign and each part of the body. Here is a translation of it in order to understand the signals your body sends you, depending on where you are suffering.

NOTE:
The more chronic the disease, the more serious the problem is, and it should be resolved as a matter of priority.

■ **Muscle system pain, headaches, and dental pain (in analogy with Aries):** difficulties in asserting oneself, acting individually, defending one's interests or expressing one's desires, leading a necessary fight, opposing others

■ **Immune-system pain, neck or throat pain (analogous to Taurus):** feeling unstable, afraid of missing something, too much greed or, on the contrary, too much deprivation, difficulty in selecting what is good for us on the outside or what may harm us

■ **Respiratory-system disorders or pain/injuries to arms and hands (analogous to Gemini):** difficulties in communicating, expressing thoughts and feelings, exchanging with one's environment, opening up to new things, people, and ideas

■ **Aches of the digestive system (in analogy with Cancer and Virgo):** difficulties in assimilating novelty in one's life, emotional injury that one cannot overcome, impossibility to appropriate a new situation, feeling of exile or abandonment, feeling of not being in one's place (intimate or social)

■ **Heart system disorders (analogous to Leo):** self-esteem injury, inability to manage the distance or disappearance of a loved one, high tension in a relationship or with children, major emotional shock

■ **Renal-system disorders (in analogy with Libra):** difficulty in cooperating with others or positioning oneself in relation to them, difficulty in finding one's place, paralyzing and painful hesitation, absence or deficiency of the filter that normally exists between oneself and others, so that the poisons of the other contaminate us

■ **Problems of the reproductive system (in analogy with Scorpio):** difficulties in sharing emotions, giving or receiving spontaneously, too much greed, difficulty in accepting changes, the end of something or simply the passing of time (deep fear of aging and death)

■ **Musculoskeletal-system disorders, especially of the hips and of the legs (in analogy with Sagittarius):** feeling of emptiness or absurdity, feeling of distraction that makes us no longer know what direction to take life—toward what, toward whom, or where to go

■ **Bone or dermal-system disorders (in analogy with Capricorn):** difficulties in structuring one's life, in making the efforts that one knows are necessary, in remaining patient, in coping with adversity, in resisting external pressures by showing oneself solid inside

■ **Nervous-system disorders (in analogy with Aquarius):** difficulties in asserting oneself as one is, in accepting or making people accept one's difference, one's originality, the feeling of being cut off from humanity, enormously disappointed by a friend

■ **Lymphatic- and hormonal-system disorders (analogous to Pisces):** difficulties in properly dosing one's behavior and balancing the different areas of one's life, in providing adequate answers to the problems encountered, in properly identifying things and situations. Psychic disorder that causes a loss of sense of identity, the desire to run away

How to relax quickly

Relaxation is not in any way contrary to attention. A small moment of real relaxation during the day is often the guarantee of prolonged attention until the evening. Here again, astrology can save us time and effort by orienting us toward the best form of relaxation according to our zodiacal dominant. Overall, this relaxation program should last between fifteen and thirty minutes to be as effective as possible.

Aries
Participate in a sport, more precisely a sport where you can let off steam, expel the nervous overload. For the less athletic, singing is also a good way to reduce pressure.

Taurus
Take time for a snack or a snack break, chewing slowly and enjoying what you eat, even if it's just an apple. You can also lovingly prepare a dish or cake.

Gemini
Go for a walk! You can also dance or do a little bit of aerobics. The main thing is to be in motion.

Cancer
Take a nap! If not, take at least a few minutes to dream quietly (by yourself or through a book or series). If you can take this break at home, it's even better.

Leo
Recharge your emotional batteries by taking a few minutes to talk to a loved one, your life partner, or your children. Ideally, hug the person. If you are alone, since you also run on solar energy, get a tan if the time is right.

Virgo

Yoga or a stretching session will relax the body and the mind. The idea is also to "reincorporate" yourself, because you often attach too much importance to your mind and goals at the expense of your body and your health.

Libra

It is by being able to talk with your usual confidant, by telling him/her about your day and by voicing your dilemmas or doubts aloud, that gets the pressure off most quickly.

Scorpio

An intimate and sensual moment would be ideal, but if this is not possible, emptying the air is also a good way to ease the pressure: devote a moment to meditation and then check off what has already been done on your to-do list.

Sagittarius

You need something that really takes your mind off things, takes you elsewhere, or makes you think of things that are totally different from your daily activity. It can be a documentary, a book, a conversation . . . Something simple that allows you to escape (and that rests the body as well as the mind!).

Capricorn

It is by isolating yourself and enjoying a quiet and peaceful environment that you will release the pressure as quickly as possible: whether you take refuge in the basement of your business, in a library, or at a yoga center does not matter much, as long as you can cut yourself off for a few minutes from the bustle and noise of the world.

Aquarius

Spending time with one or more friends—for example, by going for a coffee—is an excellent natural relaxant.

Since you are very sensitive to surrounding airwaves, try to be in the energy space of quiet people as much as you can—it has an immediate relaxing effect on you!

Pisces
Prayer and music are your two best ways to restore inner harmony. More generally, the arts and spirituality help you put down your bags and give you second wind: museums and places of worship are your favorite places to relax, unless the content of your MP3 is enough to recharge your batteries.

The essential release

Wannabe philosophers have largely scoffed at the idea of "letting go" . . . yet, it is a major lever for anyone engaged in a process of personal development: at some point, this person will have to learn to let go to allow his personality to flourish (and not *force* it to flourish, because here the will is powerless).

> **IMPORTANT**
> Letting go doesn't mean giving up on your heart's desire, or looking too deeply into the context until nothing has any value anymore.

The process of letting go is to stop the mental and emotional tension that, like a terrified child clinging to his buoy (when he has all the potential to swim freely), makes us miss out on our lives by reducing our freedom and our movements, our momentum, and our autonomy.

Without consenting to any benign behavior, letting go still requires accepting people as they are and situations as they arise, at least initially, and eventually transforming them afterward (or transforming themselves in relation to them).

Therefore, letting go is, above all, releasing our fears, our prejudices, our illusions, everything that, in a word, "plummets" our lives. Letting go is releasing ballast by putting oneself in an intellectual posture that neither rejects (*I don't want to hear about it / I don't want to talk about it*) nor grasps (*I want this or I want that*).

The role of sexuality in your balance: Sector VIII

The human being is a complex animal, and his sexuality cannot be reduced to a simple reproductive function or even a function that would be common to all. In fact, men and women live their sexuality in a certain way, and understanding what function it has in your own life can be of great help, since any blocked energy (including that called sexual) is an energy that is lacking in your normal development.

We know that there are genetic determinants that encourage people to seek intense sensations, so that some will, for example, have earlier and more active sexuality throughout their lives than others. There is also a cosmic determinant.

It is necessary to use advanced astrological techniques here (i.e., to observe a particular portion of the theme): the 8th house. If you don't know what sign your 8th house falls into, you can again use your intuition and self-analysis to guess which of the following definitions best suits you.

> **NOTE:**
> Sexuality here is called a set of behaviors and needs, ranging from physical desire to the desire for emotional sharing, eroticism, and fantasy, because if sexuality has a particular dimension for everyone, each dimension of sexuality is present, more or less, in each of us.

So let's see what's happening with regard to the astrological element that governs your 8th house:

■ **If this element is Fire** (which is the case if your sector VIII is in Aries, Leo, or Sagittarius), sex is essentially used to express your feelings and to respond to a drive (the heart prevails).

Sexuality is for you a way to vibrate in harmony with your partner, to feel together the joy and intensity of life, without guilt and even with much spontaneity in enjoyment. Sometimes it is also a pleasant way to ease everyday tensions and conflicts, to reconcile with happiness.

Be careful that your sexual excitement does not excessively influence your moods, and do not forget that the best is the enemy of good: to moderate yourself more will allow you both to be more constant in your behavior and not to experience fatigue in the bedroom.

■ **If this element is Earth** (which is the case if your sector VIII is in Taurus, Virgo, or Capricorn), sex is essentially used to express your need for affection and to respond to a sensual impulse (the senses prevail).

Sexuality is the best way for you to concretely strengthen bonds, to express your tenderness through caresses and kisses. It is a moment of closeness and trust that you like to share with a trusted person, as part of a long-term relationship.

Be careful not to self-censor (repress) your fantasies and sexual temptations felt for people other than your partner: this is not about infidelity but inhibition, because forbidding yourself to feel attraction (or being seduced by beauty) can only lead to frustration.

■ **If this element is Air** (which is the case if your sector VIII is in Gemini, Libra, or Aquarius), sex is essentially used to express your need for exchange and to respond to a surge of seduction (the spirit prevails).

Sexuality is for you largely fantasized, passing through the filter of the mind. It is about coming into contact with the intimacy of the other, communicating with the body on a transcendent plane, and a more or less conscious ultimate desire in you: to read each other's most secret thoughts.

Warning: by rationalizing, you risk taking more pleasure in seduction or foreplay rather than in the act itself, and confuse intellectual attraction and physical desire . . .

■ **If this element is Water** (which is the case if your sector VIII is in Cancer, Scorpio, or Pisces), sex is essentially used to express your need for fusion and to respond to an emotional impulse (emotions prevail).

Sexuality is for you a search for completeness and appeasement: blending into the other, forgetting yourself, abolishing limits and separations, enveloping yourself, warming yourself, protecting yourself, abandoning yourself . . .

Beware of the risk of emotional dependence; it would be better to try to build subsidiary (e.g., intellectual) interests with your partner, to avoid your relationship being built on the carnal act alone.

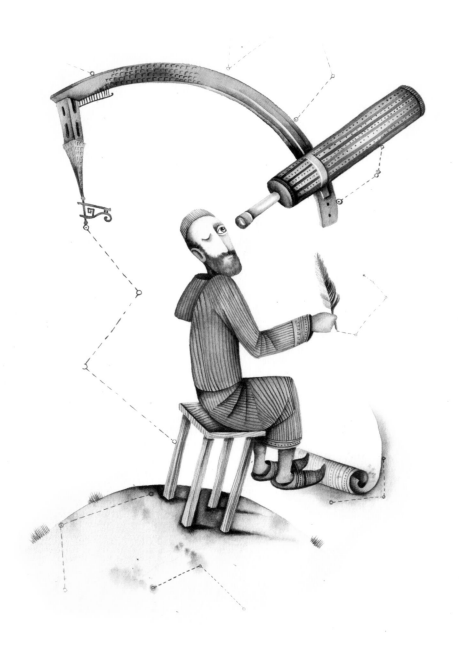

GOING TOWARD
HAPPINESS

TRANSFORM, EVOLVE, AND GROW

When nothing goes right in our lives, we may feel the need to change everything, sometimes to the point of wanting to become someone else. However, such a thing is simply not possible. So what does it mean to transform? Do we really need to change? No, of course, it is more a matter of developing, of letting your full potential shine through. Astrology, the oldest (and perhaps the wisest) of the tools for personal development, can help us do this.

> Like the course of a river, our personality hardly changes. It represents what we are meant to be. Yet, like the water of a muddy river that becomes clear and pure, we have the possibility to cleanse our personalities and purify them.
>
> —Josei Toda (Buddhist master)

Changing is not betraying oneself

Each of us has our own birth chart that accompanies us throughout our lives, just like the body given to us at birth. Moreover, like this body, our astrological theme will evolve. The baby we have been and the old person we are about to become seem very different. Yet, they are two manifestations of the same assemblage, both genetically and astrologically.

Any problem (or dissonance) in an astrological theme, if identified, can be transformed into a healthful expression of our personality. There is nothing to reject, nothing to betray; it is necessary only to readjust. Astrology starts from the premise that there is no such thing as a "bad theme" but, rather, erroneous ways (in the sense of painful for oneself or others) of living it. It is therefore a question of both evolving and becoming oneself. We can transform what is painful and unhealthful in our behavior without eliminating our personality.

Addressing dissonant aspects

Negative behaviors are indicated, in the astrological theme, by certain celestial configurations (called aspects) that can be "dissonant." The astrologer can thus quickly identify what, from birth, is likely to be a problem; that is, what can hinder happiness. There are different names for these configurations, depending on their nature (the dissonant conjunction, the square, the quincunx, and the opposition are the most important).

Let's take the example of a woman who has a dissonant configuration of Mercury and the Moon in her theme. This means that her need for security and her tendency to be curious come up against each other. Very often, she wants to go out, meet people, or discover new places, but a part of herself whispers that she would be better off staying at home, not to leave her nest, and even to stay under the duvet. If she listens to this part of herself, this woman will quickly begin to turn like a lion in a cage, will get bored, and will feel the need to chat with someone.

Although entirely internal, this kind of chronic dilemma can be very painful, since it prohibits both the development of a real sense of security (this security eventually being perceived as a prison) and a real satisfaction of one's needs for discovery (these being tainted by a feeling of insecurity and the desire to return as quickly as possible to one's protective cocoon).

However, this problem is not inevitable, and, by working on it, the person can find the right balance between external and internal life, the right balance between vagrancy and sedentary life.

The earlier the problem is recognized, the easier it will be to overcome it (this is one of the interests, for example, to have the astral theme established at the birth of a child in order to avoid, through education, reinforcing certain preexisting negativities).

It is not good, however, to be too hard or demanding on yourself: it is better to consider the less evolved parts of yourself as still infantile portions of your personality.

Thus, we will remember that in order to raise a child properly, it is necessary to show affection and patience and sometimes humor too. In the same way, self-esteem, perseverance, and self-derision are the surest ways to achieve improvement, to grow internally.

Managing desires with Mars and Venus

Desire makes the world go around. It is that, as a libido (taken in the Jungian sense; that is to say, all our desires and impulses of life, our psychological energy) that constitutes our motivation, our deep springs. We need desires to move forward, and yet, everyone has to deal with them in a certain way to avoid becoming slaves to them.

No personal-development technique worthy of the name can ignore the management of desires, and astrology is no exception—quite the contrary: no fewer than two of the most important planets in a theme are dedicated to this notion:

- Venus, which represents what we love, what we believe has value
- Mars, which represents what we are striving for, what excites us and motivates us to live

Venus and Mars are complementary, as are men and women: Venus governs our receptivity to desire (what we expect from the outside to be happy) while Mars governs our motivation to desire (what we seek from the outside to be happy).

Being able to be clear with Venus and Mars means being able to understand, accept, and manage your desires as well as possible. This is fundamental for progressing. Thus the astrologer, by studying the two planets in the theme, their positions, their aspects, can quickly detect what the desires are and gauge if they are well balanced and how they are lived.

For example, dissonances on Mars can produce frustration, which generates anger and violence, while dissonances on Venus can cause laziness and self-indulgence. In any case, it is more a question of poor integration of libido (in the broad sense previously defined) than of defects as such.

EXAMPLE:

With, in her natal chart, a dissonance of her Moon in Cancer and her Venus in Aries, Christina, divorced, feels a strong tension between her need for tranquility, domestic security, and protection of her children and her desires for love, romantic intensity, and adventure.

When she finds herself in her family's daily routine, she dreams of a prince charming kidnapping her and taking her faraway, where she lives a thousand adventures. Yet, as soon as she thinks about going on a date, making herself beautiful, wanting to awaken the flame in her, she gets afraid of anything that might compromise the peace of her home.

It is nevertheless possible for her, as for any person torn apart by this kind of inner conflict, to find the right balance. For example, by letting her heart express itself freely for an evening by really forgetting everything else (with a good babysitter as backup!) but without ever crossing the line, which will then allow her to return home in complete serenity.

What is toxic can be transformed into something healthy; the bundle of wood that you carry on your back can feed a fire of dynamism, motivation, joy of life! Thus, greed, possessiveness, addiction, and masochistic pleasures, attributable to a poorly integrated Venus, can be changed into generosity, benevolence, epicureanism, and sincere (i.e., totally unselfish) love. Similarly, the anger, aggressiveness, criticism, and sadistic pleasures of a poorly integrated Mars can become a sense of justice, constructive momentum, attention to others, and driving force.

In any case, we also gain inner freedom during this transformation because we break the chains of our conditioning; we learn to act rather than react, to give answers to others and to life rather than instinctive and, most of the time, inappropriate bursts.

The notion of well-being with the Moon

As for the Moon, we refer the reader to our previous book, *Les Pouvoirs bénéfiques de la Lune*, published by Mango Editions, in which we develop in detail the effects of the night star.

Let us simply remember here that if we consider the movement of the planets as a kind of cosmic clock, the Moon would be the smallest hand, the one that indicates the moods and daily oscillations of our lives.

Its influence isn't often very strong, but it is regular and constant, and its proper consideration in our lives helps us manage daily astral influences.

The Moon also concerns our emotional life, and we can therefore imagine how its influence helps us avoid being swamped by fleeting feelings that are as changeable as the phases of the Moon.

Break free of mind conditioning with Mercury

Growing up and developing involves getting rid of your old skin at some point or leaving clothes that have become too tight. In other words, to abandon our habits, our automatisms, our psychological models — in short, in a word: our conditioning. Whether cultural or family, induced by society or by our close environment, conditioning denies who we really are, and freeing ourselves from it is therefore a necessary step toward a broader liberation of our deep identity.

There are different types of conditioning, and it is quite easy to identify which one dominates in a person, depending on their theme and more particularly on the planet Mercury. Depending on its position in relation to the Sun, three main types can be identified. If you do not know this information, read the following descriptions carefully; you should be able to discern which category you belong to (perhaps with the advice of a few benevolent relatives, however, since it is difficult to perceive your own conditioning).

NOTE:
In 1909, physicist Thomas Young conducted an experiment on photons that concluded that a human being was capable, by the power of his attention alone, of influencing reality to the point of changing its nature. How can what is true on the outside not be true all the more so on the inside? By observing yourself carefully, you are already starting to improve . . .

It should be noted that these are trends that have been deliberately magnified to better identify them. As part of a complete study of an astrological birth chart, these data are of course nuanced and enriched.

■ **If Mercury is after the Sun in the order of the zodiac,** your main conditioning is inattention. We can also talk about distraction or, at its highest level, an "I don't care" attitude.

In any case, your main conditioning makes you partly hermetic to the world around you; you do not always notice what is happening, let alone what people feel or express around you.

You often forget to do things (especially chores), or you do them at the last minute, in haste and confusion, no longer having a choice.

It is not uncommon for you to lose small items or not remember where you put them (your keys or your mobile phone, for example).

You often seem to be dreaming, lost in thought, sometimes even drowsy or apathetic. You do a lot of things on autopilot, without thinking about it, because you lack investment in the real world, subjects and activities that simply do not interest you.

You prefer your reflection, your imagination, or sources of external distractions (such as a song, an animal, etc.) at the expense of paying attention to what you are doing, if it isn't fun or stimulating enough.

■ **If Mercury is before the Sun in the order of the zodiac,** your main conditioning is denial.

You may have something staring you in the face, but you have the greatest difficulty believing it because you have strong opinions on many subjects, including those of which you have only theoretical experience.

Your thoughts somehow precede your life; you have prejudices and can deny evidence just because reality contradicts your assumptions; it is sometimes not as logical or interesting as the idea you have of it.

You are an idealist par excellence; what you believe often takes precedence over what you experience, and you can go as far as fanaticism because it is nothing more than idealism taken to the extreme. Thus, you are able to love madly (and despite common sense), believe immeasurably in a religion or cause (however bad), be blinded by hope, and stubbornly pursue the same path (yet condemned in advance if you carried out a thorough analysis of your situation).

Faced with a situation or a person that does not suit you, you will seek to drive them out, to make them disappear from your life (and especially from your mind), rather than make the effort to integrate, accept, and assimilate them.

■ **If Mercury is in close conjunction with the Sun,** your main conditioning is subjectivity.

We could say that your perception of reality is distorted from the outset, biased by a systematic interpretation of the world according to your feelings, your criteria, and your moods. Things are not as they are; they are as they seem to you, and, in that sense, you can show exceptional bad faith, telling everyone that the snow is gray because you don't see it differently with your sunglasses on your nose.

Your reality prevails over reality, and you can therefore conceive the world in a very personal and totally illusory way, thinking that what is true for you is universally true, which can lead you, if you have any power at all, to be authoritarian and unfair. Moreover, since your judgment is biased, we cannot essentially expect anything objective from you. All your understanding of the world and others passes through the filter of your emotions and feelings, and you have the greatest difficulty in really putting yourself in the shoes of others or accepting a different point of view.

Whatever the case, don't forget that no conditioning is irreparable: on the contrary, one can drive out conditioning in an instant, with a deep and sincere awareness. Of course, it will then take time to set up a more healthful way of perceiving life, this will have to be done very gradually, but at the very moment when we perceive a conditioning process, a transformation process immediately begins.

NOTE:
Research in quantum physics teaches us that the observer changes the nature of what he observes. However, in terms of personal development, the observer and the observed are one and the same: by simply becoming aware of who we are, we can begin to change our deepest nature.

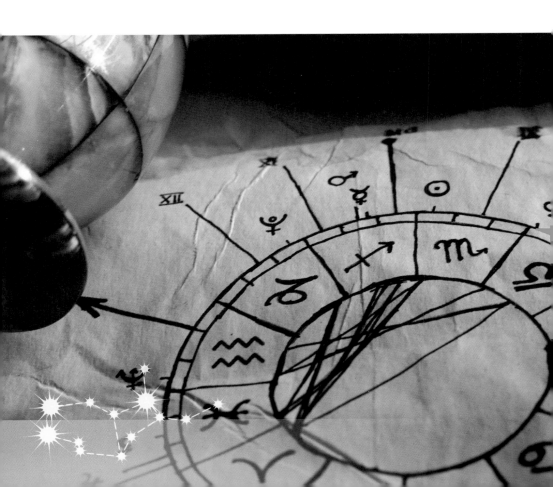

Facing suffering and difficulties through one's birth chart

When the mind is troubled, the multiplicity of things takes over; when the mind is quiet, multiplicity disappears before Unity.

—Ashvagosha (Indian philosopher and poet)

In a way, our astrological theme can be seen as a wonderful diagnostic shortcut, since it is a synthesis of our psychology. We see all our potential, assets, and handicaps. We can guess the expression of symptoms and, if they are proven, understand their root causes. Then we can find solutions, a way forward that does not consist of bypassing what is problematic but of integrating it so that it is no longer a problem. Because basically, it's all about interior integration.

Faced with the suffering we encounter, we can either flee from it or decide to face it. Flight weakens us, makes us even more afraid of the next pain, while fighting allows us to develop.

Suffering and pain: What's the difference?

Pain is inevitable and external: it can be physical (burning, hunger), relational (unwanted separation, big argument), psychological (humiliation, rejection), social (loss of job, racism), circumstantial (grief, theft), or multiple (rape, for example, generates a triple physical, relational, and psychological pain, to which social pain can be added if the victim is accused of having provoked her aggressor).

Suffering is inner and avoidable: in a way, it's the consequence of poor pain management (integration) that adds mental (subjective) pain to the initial (objective) pain. For example, if I am fired, I can choose to get on with my life, to show hope and confidence without looking back (the social pain is there, but I will do everything to overcome it quickly). On the other hand, I can ruminate against injustice, dwell on everything that has happened in recent months, complain, and get angry (the pain is amplified by the reaction I have toward it).

The study of our astrological theme can be of great help to us, on the one hand, by allowing us to identify our strengths and weaknesses, and, on the other hand, by regaining confidence in our latent potential while accepting our imperfections and the blows that life deals us.

This way we can understand what is happening to us and why it is happening (this idea is developed in the following pages). In some cases, if a third person is included, we are better able to assess that person's motivations and behaviors. The study of our theme finally allows us, if necessary, to (re)focus on our most important long-term objectives by considering the present as a stage, a simple step on which we could stumble while climbing the stairs of our destiny.

Surpassing yourself with higher octaves

> *Experience is not what happens to man; it is what man does with what happens to him.*
>
> —Aldous Huxley (British writer)

Astrology informs us individually about our possibilities of "transcendence" (i.e., personal surpassing or transformation from above). This concerns, among other things, an astrological notion that is little known to the public in general: that of upper octaves. Faced with a difficulty affecting our "little ego" and the functions related to it (our thoughts with Mercury, our affects with Venus, our desires and wills with Mars), we can decide to raise the debate and to float above our problems by approaching them with our "greater self": that is, with distance, wisdom, and nobility.

When we go through a storm, we can choose to simply hold on, hang in there, stay the course, and wait for things to calm down. But we can also choose to rise like a plane above the clouds to avoid turbulence. We then move on to the upper octave of our lives.

In the astral chart, three planetary pairs, each representing a basic function and its superior version, indicate this possibility:

■ The feelings, attachments, and loves proper to Venus can be broadened through Neptune into a much-broader compassion and love, no longer focusing simply on what we love or not but on life in general.

■ Our thoughts and conceptions and our opinions (Mercury) can be transfigured through Uranus, which will help us think, much more in terms of humanity than in terms of the individual, about solutions beneficial to the greatest number of people rather than just us.

■ Our wills (Mars) can also be enhanced through Pluto, planet par excellence of the collective unconscious, able to make us discover impulses of life and conquest much deeper than those consisting simply of trying to satisfy our individual desires.

With Pluto, it is the whole of humanity that is sought to be fulfilled by pulling society toward objectives that are beneficial to all. We will have understood that the astrological system has in its very structure the idea of going beyond our limited ego to develop—according to Carl Gustav Jung's terminology—a greater Self; that is to say, psychical entirety.

This is, in the end, the objective of all personal-development work, the word "personal" not meaning a withdrawal into oneself but, on the contrary, the idea that by developing each person fully reintegrates his place within the human community, by going beyond the narrow limits of his ego.

NOTE:
By studying the reciprocal positions of Venus/Neptune, Mars/ Pluto, and Mercury/Uranus, the astrologer will be able to give many keys to transcendence to anyone who is ready to receive them.

DEVELOP OVER TIME

The supremacy of astrology over all other personal-development techniques is based on respect for time. It is indeed very useful to identify one's talents, disabilities, and potentials, but it is even more useful to know how to harmonize with the flow of the universe and do the right thing at the right time.

Integrate the notion of a cycle (the ages of life)

No other approach allows this adjustment to the right timing, which translates into two major astrological notions: planetary cycles and planetary transits and progressions.

The planetary cycles

With regard to cycles, we can also talk about a very deep highlighting of the different stages of life, and the key moments that mark our existence. It is therefore possible to detect a temporal structure in human existence. We can indeed observe (and experience) the tonality that the movement of the planets causes, at certain specific times, in relation to the position they occupied at the time of birth.

Since the planets move at a speed known to each of them (this is what we call in astronomy the "planetary step"), we can establish a kind of existential calendar highlighting important milestones in the course of our lives.

These periods are the same for everyone, but each one will live them in his own way according to his temperament, his history, and his personal evolution, but also the whole of his birth chart.

It is this difference in experience that makes the phenomenon, although universal, not easy to identify; but if you know what to look for, you will easily discover the nature of these periods and, in doing so, the common experience that unites everyone of the same age.

Note that what follows is a brief and crude summary of the concept of the planetary cycle. We mention only the most-important cycles, but others more subtle also punctuate the ages of life (such as every twelve years, the return of Jupiter to its birth position).

In the planetary cycle, the information is interpreted in relation to the rest of the astral theme and the person's background. However, the phases have a general dimension that can be explained as follows.

Around seven years old (first square of Saturn)
It is the first key step toward adulthood, the first major challenge of maturity: we leave early childhood. At school, you enter the first grade; you are with "the big kids" (an abusive expression, but nevertheless very representative of the experience you have had).

There's no longer a question of spending your time playing; you have to start learning, disciplining, making efforts, concentrating. At worst, we have our first experiences of disability, frustration, and rejection. At best, we discover our first satisfactions in relation to self-discipline and the increase of personal capacities, and you become less dependent on your family.

Around fourteen years old (Saturn's first opposition)
In astrology, this phase corresponds to the true beginning of adolescence and its own oppositions (to parents, school and social systems, rivals in love). Basically, it is a crisis of identity, a difficulty in situating oneself in the world, in taking one's place. First, we define ourselves "against" things and people. Our body itself seems to be playing "against us," since it is changing against our will, and the transition is rarely easy to live with.

At worst, one can feel very alone (alone in the world) and helpless in the face of life, the pressure of society, biology (sleep, digestion, hormones), family. At best, we become more aware of the reality of life, and we have foundational experiences (first loves, first professional orientations).

Around twenty-one years old (second square of Saturn)

Formerly the age of majority in France, this key period corresponds to the finalization of the maturity process that began around the age of seven, during the first square. We are now an adult, or at least we are considered as such by society.

It is a good idea to seek more independence and freedom (some will start working, while others will take a room on the campus, for example), to assert ourselves more as an autonomous person and be able to take care of our own needs (or at least to strive for them).

At worst, you feel unable to support yourself and find the path you need, which causes suffering and depression. At best, we gain even more realism, we strengthen our self-confidence, and we affirm more who we are and what we want to do with our lives.

Around twenty-six years old (Neptune's first sextile)

It is a privileged moment to become aware of our belonging to the world and to integrate ourselves more through a social, cultural, professional, or artistic ideal.

It can be the end of long studies and entry into professional life, membership in a movement, or commitment to a cause. In any case, it is good to get involved in something collective, to feel the dimensions of your life expanding.

Around twenty-nine years old (Saturn's first return to its native position)
This is the time for a first assessment of your life: you are old enough to look back on your past, to look at what you have already accomplished and what remains to be done. It is a time that should be devoted to redetermining oneself, strengthening one's will, and giving a constructive impetus to one's life. Some may, for example, decide to start a family, others may change jobs, and some may move or discover a new passion.

In any case, we are now obliged to take into account the factor of time, the management of the years that pass: many people only really start to become aware of the notion of aging at this pivotal moment in their lives.

At worst, you may feel like you have failed, wasted time, that you are imprisoned in a life that does not suit you, or are weighed down by obligations (family, professional). At best, we find a new breath, we optimize our time management by setting our priorities better, and we make the big decisions that used to frighten us until now but that we feel strong enough to face today.

Around thirty-six years old (third square of Saturn)
Period in symbolic echo with our seven-year age (first square of Saturn); once again, life offers us the chance to begin a new stage of inner growth, of maturity (which normally should bring us this time to wisdom).

The question of our place in society and our role in life in general arises again. At worst, one can feel very isolated and overwhelmed by duties or constraints (e.g., marital, family, professional). At best, we can better understand and assume our responsibilities, enjoy taking on new challenges, and become a pillar for others.

EXAMPLE:
With her Saturn in Leo, Melanie was an unwanted child, and, because of the often-indifferent or devaluing treatment she received when she was growing up, she had lacked self-confidence in her potential (see p. 64, "Your basic deficiency, becoming resilient with Saturn").

During her early thirties, she worked hard to get to know herself better, but at the age of thirty-five she went through a very painful love separation that made her lose all desire to live for several months. A year later, she was over it and, encouraged by the advice of her astrologer, decided to go for broke by starting her own small business of handcrafted jewelry (which her former partner, far too eager to keep her under his control, had always dissuaded her from doing).

This company was successful and reconciled Melanie with the idea of personal victory, proving to herself that she was capable of achieving something on her own, and helping her, beyond the financial aspect of things, to consolidate her identity and will.

Around forty-four years old (second opposition of Saturn)
This period is a symbolic echo of our teenage crisis at fifteen years old (Saturn's first opposition). It is often referred to as the "midlife crisis," and for good reason: we are asking ourselves again who we are, what we want from life, and how we can achieve it in practice. The feeling of aging may become more acute with some more or less severe health alerts, or simply accentuation marks of time: wrinkles, gray hair . . .

Often, it is useful to "oppose" others once more in order to better differentiate, find each other, restructure. Broken marriages are numerous at this age, as are conflicts with children, who are often teenagers or young adults.

At worst, we feel an intense adversity (e.g., in our home, our work) as if the world was gathering against us and we were unable to do anything other than suffer. At best, we refocus our energies on a limited number of objectives, eliminating those that have become impossible (as in the case of maternity for women) or getting rid of the superfluous or those who limit our potential.

Around forty-eight years old (first trine of Neptune)

Echoing Neptune's sextile (at twenty-six years old), it is a question of abandoning new objectives that are too personal or selfish to contribute more to collective projects, dynamics that go beyond our "little self," and consist of participating in the evolution of the world (and in particular the quality of life of future generations).

It is good in such a period not to lose sight of the fact that the future is created every day, and that everyone contributes to it on their own scale, including in the most-modest acts (for example, in our purchases or the ideas that we convey daily and that we participate in spreading).

Around fifty-one years old (fourth square of Saturn)

This period calls for renewal by redefining our way of acting or our goals. We have to take into account the body's aging process and adapt our life and work in function to it. It is no longer possible to just "continue as before": it is now necessary to consider certain biological but also spiritual imperatives: this is the moment, if we have not already done so, to begin a spiritual quest, to cultivate a philosophical dimension, because the older we get, the more we should feel the impermanence of all that is material (our body as well as our external wealth).

At worst, it is difficult to draw an assessment of our past; we lack perspective on our lives and can therefore feel limited by the burdens we face on a daily basis (the credits contracted, the children who cause problems and still need help, the irascible spouse . . .). At best, we really gain deeper wisdom, which allows us to reorganize our life with lucidity, on the basis of actual priorities and opportunities.

Around fifty-nine years old (Saturn's second return to her native position)

For some lucky people, it is already retirement age, and for many others, it is the age where we think more and more about it! We feel that this is an important transition period during which we have the opportunity to free ourselves of the past, but with the important question "What to do with my future?" unanswered.

Many situations can naturally end, and it is necessary to take stock to look to the future. We can also be reminded of some of the conditions we have already met and have the chance to experience, them differently, with more maturity and wisdom (for example, many people who assume the role of grandparents or train a successor at work or rethink friendships).

At worst, you may feel bitterness and frustration with some people, wishes not fulfilled, but it is never too late to do well. At best, we begin to accumulate a strong existential experience, and we seriously ask ourselves the questions "What use is it going to be?" and "How best to transmit it?"

Around sixty-seven years old (fifth square of Saturn)

This period symbolically echoes our seventh and thirty-sixth years (respectively, first and third squares of Saturn). Life again proposes a stage of inner growth, of maturity, which should allow us to deepen our wisdom. The question of our place in society and our role in life in general is once more called into question. When you are no longer working, when the children are autonomous and have left home, what meaning should you give to your life?

At worst, you can feel very lonely, desperate because your life seems aimless, sometimes limited by an aging body.

At best, one may want to take up new challenges and find a new social role; for example, through associations (e.g., cultural, charitable), civic or political engagement, the development of creative skills (e.g., writing, painting), or the transmission of knowledge (on a family, local, or higher level).

Around seventy-five years old (third opposition of Saturn)

This period is the symbolic echo of the adolescent crisis (first opposition of Saturn) and the midlife crisis (second opposition). Often underestimated, the weight of years is felt, health alerts are more frequent, and we are physically capable of less and less . . . yet, the message of any Saturnine opposition is the same: it is time to "oppose" others again to better differentiate, find, and restructure ourselves.

There are many separations (including death or hospitalization), as well as conflicts (although theoretically "smoothed" by the wisdom of age) with our children and grandchildren (who are often at the ungrateful age of adolescence or having difficulties at the beginning of working life). Socially, it is often the moment when we are called upon to defend the old world, the one we have experienced, in the face of little judicious progress made.

At worst, one can become very reactionary by clinging to what has been, refusing any evolution and criticizing all those who think differently. We can lock ourselves in the past, cultivating nostalgia because we no longer "find ourselves" in the present world, which even seems very hostile to us. At best, we can contribute to the preservation and transmission of knowledge and experience, setting an example by remaining young in spirit and encouraging our grandchildren, helping them as best we can. By redefining some medium- and short-term goals, you can make things happen that you really want (for example, take a trip you've been dreaming of for a long time, or moving home to be closer to your family).

Around eighty-two years old (sixth square of Saturn)

This is a period that invites us to reorganize our lives by taking into account our aging and declining capacities for autonomy.

The emphasis should be on spiritual life and metaphysical issues around life and death. The central question seems to be "What will I leave to the world, to others, to my family, and how will I do it?"

At worst, one can obviously feel overwhelmed by the years, too old for anything, a prisoner in a body that doesn't obey one as it once did. At best, one achieves true wisdom and organizes the end of our life with clarity, according to real priorities and possibilities.

Around ninety years old (Saturn's last return to her native position)
Those who reach this beautiful age experience a new and important transition period during which they have the opportunity to free themselves from the past and to consider with great depth and foresight everything that may have happened to them in life, understanding how everything has been useful and favorable (this work can of course be done long before by those who undertake a personal-development process early in their lives!).

Many situations and people previously known disappear or have already disappeared. However, we can get to know some of the conditions that have already been met, and have the chance to experience them differently, with more maturity and wisdom (for example, many people in the role of great-grandparents).

At worst, one can feel great wear and tear, great fatigue, and the desire for it to end. At best, one has achieved the status of "wise" with others and can be a valuable witness to the previous decades.

The right thing at the right time
It is good to know what to do and, even better, when to do it. For this reason, astrology constitutes an irreplaceable tool for personal development, since the study of transits and progressions, linked to the birth chart, will allow everyone, in a very individual way, to concentrate on certain particular areas of life, according to the accentuation of the astrological sectors by the running of the stars. One could say that astrology is the science of good timing, or the wisdom of *kairos*.

The notion of *kairos* was developed by the ancient Greeks but remains relevant today. *Kairos* is the time of opportunity, the time when an opportunity arises and can be seized, if sufficient discernment is exercised.

WHY KAIROS?

The Greek god Kairos, likened to both good fortune and good idea, was a young man with a large tuft of hair. When opportunity appeared, one could either let it pass or "grab it by the hair": the expression has stayed with us.

By drawing the practitioner's attention to one field of life rather than another, astrology therefore makes it possible, in the literal sense, to orient the people, to channel their efforts in a specific direction rather than letting them disperse and tilt at windmills, rather than wasting their energy (which happens, in a way, when we privilege a subject that is not "on the cosmic agenda").

The study of dynamic astrology (see p. 36) makes it possible to locate oneself in time as a road map makes it possible in space, because one of the most precious teachings of astrology is to confirm (and prove) that there is indeed "a time for everything." Knowing how to dedicate the right period of life to the right field of existence (for example, struggling for work when necessary or, on the contrary, knowing when to stop working to create a family) is, in the end, one of the secrets of a happy life, because vitality is then used optimally; since we are "on the right slope," on the right path, our life naturally follows an inclination, "rails" that make things easier at that moment rather than another.

EXAMPLE:

For several months, Jean-Marc experienced the transit of Saturn in his sector I, a sector that tells us about our body. Overweight for years, he made the decision, thanks to this astral movement and with the advice of his astrologer, to tackle his obesity for the umpteenth time (several diets had previously failed, resulting in even greater overweight). Armed with a renewed determination and because the right time had come, he found a nutritionist whose innovative approach corresponded to his needs and, in the period of Saturn's transit (a little over two years in his case), he lost some 25 kilos... Is it worth mentioning that feeling good in his body is an essential step in his personal development?

Transits and progressions

Thus, to understand what the splendid domains are, at the different periods of our lives, we will first try to understand Jupiter's movements through the sectors of our theme. The good news is that for those who know how to look, there is always at least one area of splendor, whatever the moment of our lives, even the darkest (this is essential information for renewing hope!).

Then we will study Saturn's transits to understand the domain of life that requires the most effort and patience at a given moment, of endurance, but which can also be consolidated and contribute to our future security, if we know how to use its qualities.

Finally, we will look more particularly at Uranus's path to know the area of life in which a specific effort of originality or liberation should be made.

All the planets, in their revolutions around the zodiac, teach us, and the combination of these different influences allows the professional to establish an astral calendar in order to advise us week by week.

In parallel and in addition, the astrologer also uses what are called progressions, whose principle is to draw equivalences between days and years.

Finally, he can still complete his range of techniques by using the solar-revolution process, which takes place every year at the time of our anniversary (but which, on the other hand, should never be interpreted alone).

Understand the meaning of events (related to transits)

Men, at times, are masters of their own fate; and if our condition is low,
it is not our stars that are to blame, it is ourselves.

—William Shakespeare (excerpt from Julius Caesar)

It seems obvious that as long as we consider life as a succession of blind accidents, it seems both absurd and cruel. Astrology can bring about a profound revolution in our conception of things, our philosophy of life, because whoever has taken the time to study it sufficiently, or to have recourse to the services of a competent professional, understands that on the contrary, everything has a meaning, and nothing in our lives happens precisely "by chance."

If the notion of planetary age already makes it possible to draw a structure of life common to any individual, the astrologer can go much further by analyzing the birth chart. Not only does everyone have a kind of starting point and an end point to reach in his life (a karmic line; see p. 148, "Working on your karma"), but your birth chart constitutes a certain interface between the universe and you, which informs us about the individual skeleton of your life.

However, it should not be misunderstood that the latter is "predictive." This is a misconception that has profoundly damaged astrology. It makes forecasts—not predictions, it says what could happen and what it means, but it never says what will happen. It is a statistic, not a fatality; it works according to probabilities, not certainties.

As a practitioner, I am also in the habit of including in the introduction to all my predictive studies a clear warning on this subject, stipulating that astrology describes climates, trends, currents that take us in one direction or another; these directions may suit us or displease us but often represent necessary passages in our lives.

However, the human being, endowed with free will, influences the stars as much as the stars influence him. Therefore, no forecast can be inevitable (good or bad), because our actions, our choices, and our decisions will be just as important as the planetary transits.

Thus, good influxes can be transformed into happy events only if the person puts his or her heart into it (if the stars promise a professional success to a person, for example, this will happen only if the person makes efforts in this direction).

Similarly, hard influxes can be corrected and become profitable (in the more or less medium term) if the person knows how to adapt and react as well as possible to what the stars offer him.

NOTE:
Our existence is clearly subject to two distinct energies: the first comes from the outside and is astrological; the second comes from the inside and is individual. To have recourse to an astrologer is precisely to have understood the importance of reconciling these two energies as well as possible in order to make them a powerful and fulfilling synergy.

The stars therefore represent an environment in its own right (just like the social, family, or national environment), on which we interact and which is more or less favorable depending on the type of action we take. Thus, each planet, as it moves, will activate one or more elements of our natal chart and create a certain trend, a beam of possibility. For example, Venus will create cohesion or, on the contrary, disharmony in our life, while Uranus will always bring renewal (in the shape of good or bad surprises).

However, beyond the raw fact, it is especially important to understand its meaning. If Uranus is placed in such a way that the probability of a breakup is very high, there is nothing gratuitous or unfair about it.

We can realize this if we take enough distance from our lives to judge with hindsight what is happening to us (see p. 117, "Facing suffering and difficulties through one's birth chart").

There is no standard answer: it depends on the theme of each, but the purpose of a divorce caused by Uranus for example, may occur to restore freedom from which our partner deprived us, or to allow us to pursue new objectives, to take a new direction (which, if we know how to follow it, will always lead us, in the end, to a better life).

NOTE:
Understanding the meaning of events makes it possible to accept them by placing them in the overall scenario of our existence. This acceptance can bring us the serenity that, in turn, will allow us to continue our inner growth.

AWAKEN YOUR OWN WISDOM

As long as you try to be something other than what you really are, your mind exhausts itself. But if you say to yourself, "This is what I am, this is a fact that I will examine and understand," then you can go beyond that.

—Krishnamurti (Indian sage)

Evolve by becoming more oneself (the ascendant)

Apart from the sun sign, the ascendant is one of the best-known notions of astrology. It asserts itself with age and even becomes more and more important over time. I tend to say that the ascendant represents the best that can be developed in each of us (in addition to the qualities and assets that exist elsewhere in the birth chart and that are "innate"): it therefore occupies a very special place in the journey of a person in search of himself and of domestic growth.

The ascendant contains the qualities that help us grow and allow us to access the entirety of our potential. During a first astrological consultation, it is always important to evaluate where the person stands in relation to his ascendant: Is he normally developed for his age? On the contrary, does he seem suffocated, inhibited? In this case, it is likely that the entire human development of the person is also blocked, sometimes for years!

Here is a small self-assessment test to assess the good development of your ascendant. Note that if you are under twenty-eight years of age, it is normal that some features are missing. On the contrary, if you are over forty years old and certain aspects of your ascendant are still not expressed in your daily life, it is likely that a problem exists, that a blockage stagnates your normal evolution.

Between these two ages, you can say that you are in the process, and the following lines can help you complete it.

If you are an Aries ascendant
You have had to learn, are learning, or will learn in the near future to show more courage and initiative, independence, and fighting spirit. The lesson of your ascendant is to understand that what matters is to be a fully fledged individual.

If you are a Taurus ascendant
You have had to learn, are learning, or will learn in the near future to be more stable and kind, affectionate, and realistic. The lesson of your ascendant is to understand that what matters is to be true to your values.

If you are a Gemini ascendant
You have had to learn, are learning, or will learn in the near future to show more curiosity and generosity of mind, sociability, and reasoning. The lesson of your ascendant is to understand that what matters is openness to the outside world.

If you are a Cancer ascendant
You have had to learn, are learning, or will learn in the near future to show more sensitivity and tenderness, imagination, and dedication to loved ones. The lesson of your ascendant is to understand that what matters is the accentuation of intimate life.

If you are a Leo ascendant
You have had to learn, are learning, or will learn in the near future to show a more personal affirmation and authority, generosity, and protective spirit. The lesson of your ascendant is to understand that what matters is the free expression of what you think and feel.

If you are a Virgo ascendant

You have had to learn, are learning, or will learn in the near future to be more reflective and logical, balanced, and effective. The lesson of your ascendant is to understand that what matters is what you will actually be able to do.

If you are Libra ascendant

You have had to learn, are learning, or will learn in the near future to show more diplomacy and dialogue, understanding, and consensus. The lesson of your ascendant is to understand that what matters is harmony with the outside world.

If you are a Scorpio ascendant

You have had to learn, are learning, or will learn in the near future to show more questioning and depth of mind, passion, and a taste for challenge. The lesson of your ascendant is to understand that what matters is to take change and adversity as engines of life.

If you are a Sagittarius ascendant

You have had to learn, are learning, or will learn in the near future to show more tolerance and a spirit of synthesis, commitment, and philosophy. The lesson of your ascendant is to understand that only a broad vision of the world allows us to truly understand it.

If you are a Capricorn ascendant

You have had to learn, are learning, or will learn in the near future to demonstrate a sense of duty and a taste for responsibility, ambition, and wisdom. The lesson of your ascendant is to understand that what matters is our contribution to society.

If you are an Aquarius ascendant

You have had to learn, are learning, or will learn in the near future to show more fraternity and a spirit of cooperation, eccentricity, and love for the new.

The lesson of your ascendant is to understand that what matters is to participate in the evolution of things.

If you are a Pisces ascendant
You have had to learn, are learning, or will learn in the near future to show more concern and empathy, universal consciousness, and faith. The lesson of your ascendant is to understand that what matters most belongs to the invisible and depends on our soul.

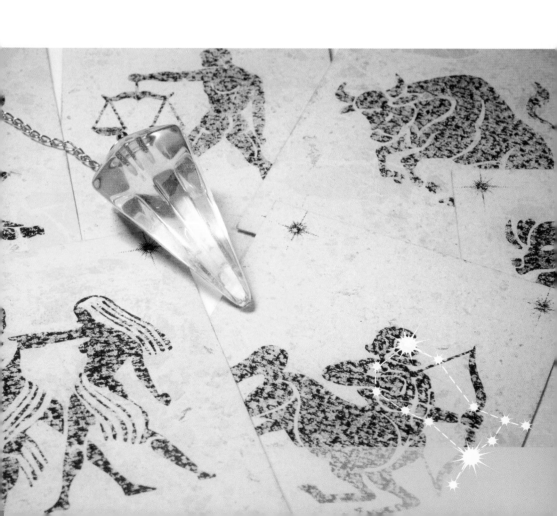

Astrology, a just existence, and cosmic order

Since humans have been thinking about the best way to be happy, we can say that only five great answers have been given by the greatest minds:

■ **The religious response** (monotheism), which consists of being in the obedience of God or the divinities of Nature (animism, polytheism, shamanism, or even ancestor worship)

■ **The humanist response** (since the Enlightenment), which consists of participating in progress, encouraging it on a scientific and technological level

■ **The philosophical response** (especially with Nietzsche and his followers), which consists of freeing oneself from all illusions and conditioning to be truly free individuals

■ **The modern response** (especially with nonviolence movements and the hippie movement), which consists of developing and spreading love

■ And perhaps the oldest answer, which we owe in particular to the ancient Greeks and which remains the most relevant, which can be described as **cosmogony**, which consists of being happy by putting ourselves in harmony with the natural Order of the World, of the Universe. This answer is also, of course, astrology, which makes it possible, in a way, to put the individual back into his environment and to enlighten him on his right place, his right role in this great Whole.

We have seen many uses of the natal chart in the pages of this book, but we are in fact very far from having covered them, because astrology has been growing for more than two thousand years at least, and its resources sometimes seem infinite. For example, we could talk about the importance of "angles" in the astrological theme. These angles, called Descendants, Middle of Heaven, or Bottom of Heaven, inform each of us about his right place (meaning the best for his happiness) within his couple, in his professional career and in his family, respectively. The study of the Sun and Moon in the theme, on the other hand, can be used to better understand the inner images we have of the roles of man and woman. The notion of axis informs us about the "right balance" that we must seek in this or that area of our lives.

> **NOTE:**
> Astrology is in any case the ideal tool for personal development to match the wonderful law that exists wherever there is life; it allows us to adjust to life rather than to fight it.

Work on your karma (karmic astrology)

When people wake up to their true mission in life, they can solve all the problems they encounter.

—Leon Tolstoy

Talking about karma in a book about personal development may seem off topic or even contradictory. That is not the case. However, it is necessary to agree on the notion of karma, since the use of this term is not in any way deterministic (such as "everything is already written at birth") or fatalistic ("whatever must happen can't be changed ").

First, let us give a very simple definition: karma is the result of our actions and thoughts. This is true, with quite a lot of evidence in the course of our current life (what we have done since our birth has an impact on what we are and are doing today), and this is true, less obviously but just as logical, from one life to the next.

In other words, the consequences of our actions do not "disappear" at the moment of our death, and we will have to reap what we have sown at one time or another, when a situation (a transit) "awakens" this karma. What we do with it at that time, however, will depend on our state of mind: we can therefore change any karma by adopting a position of wisdom.

EXAMPLE

For example, if your karma causes you to be swindled (because you have previously been greedy and unscrupulous yourself), you can either stoically accept the thing (while seeking justice through legal channels, which is normal) or tell yourself that since the world is full of thieves, there is no reason why you should not steal too (reproduction of karma) or seek revenge; for example, by brutalizing the cheat (production of a violent karma). In any case, it is your current reaction that will produce the erasure of bad karma through its reproduction or transformation into another type of karma, just as problematic, if not more so.

The most effective way to change your karma, to free yourself from it, and therefore, in terms of personal development, to become as autonomous and free as possible, is to adopt an approach to life that is full of depth and wisdom. In other words, by changing the inner cause (yourself, your reactions), you can profoundly change the general course of your life.

The so-called karmic astrology is specialized in this kind of background analysis, but in practice it is not an exclusively esoteric application of astrology: the goal is always to allow everyone, through a good understanding of the phenomena and functioning of the universe, to succeed in freeing themselves from their repetitive thought patterns and deepest conditioning (those of karmic origin being by essence the most ancient, going back to one or more existences).

Even better: karmic astrology can also help us define the type of mission that justifies our incarnation (why we came to Earth). We reach here the highest degree of astrological practice, as well as its most exciting level, since our astral chart is also able to define, for those who know how to make it speak, the meaning of our life, its purpose. What more valuable personal development tool can you offer someone? For it is only to the extent that our lives are driven by the right purpose that we can develop to our maximum potential: there is a match between our optimal growth and the achievement of a karmic goal, the realization of our earthly mission.

You could say that a bird can't fully deploy his wings until it knows where to fly . . .

CONCLUSION
& SHORT ASTROLOGICAL LEXICON

CONCLUSION

The type of personal development offered by astrology does not consist of a vain approach to conforming to a prefabricated model. It is a transformation of what is dark in us into its luminous side: nothing is useless, and nothing is to be rejected as long as we have the will to work on ourselves, to become better.

Personal development through astrology allows us to have access to our full potential, to experience every event, good or bad, as an experience of growth, to broaden our consciousness, and, finally, to raise our state of life.

Let us recall Carl Gustav Jung's approach: it is not a question of achieving perfection but of achieving totality. We can also say that it is a question of putting the segment of the universe that we are in, in the place that best suits it, with those who feed it best, in the role where it can flourish and make its most significant contribution.

A well-understood astrology, used in a modern way with the reinforcement of the knowledge in psychology accumulated during the last century, is not the vehicle of any fatality: on the contrary, it is an instrument of evolution.

Evolution or revolution? In astrology we often speak of "planetary revolution" (the advance of a planet through its orbit), which leads us to the concept of "human revolution" (the advance of an individual through his life). A human revolution is a revolution of the conscience. In addition, since we all live on the same planet, and since we are all connected, changing leads others to do the same. In this way, we create a fundamental movement.

If a person changes, everything changes. If a single touch of paint is modified, the whole painting is affected. Each person is the starting point for ten thousand others and contains in infinitesimal quantity all that constitutes the universe.

To devote oneself to one's personal development leads indirectly to the improvement of the world: those who do not lose sight of this idea can enlarge their potential, their heart, and their life on an unsuspected scale.

Astrology gives us a very important message: a brilliant sun exists deep inside each of us. Moreover, the entire universe is contained in the heart of a single person. How, therefore, can we not find enough space for everyone?

SHORT ASTROLOGICAL LEXICON OF PERSONAL DEVELOPMENT

Aspect

Relationship between two points of the astrological theme. Depending on the respective position of the bodies envisaged, an aspect may be tense, disharmonic, unpleasant to live, or, on the contrary, relaxed, harmonious, pleasant.

Element

There are four elements in astrology: Fire, Earth, Air, and Water. Each sign of the zodiac belongs to one of these elements, and each element represents a certain number of temperaments that we find in all the signs belonging to it (see pp. 28, 42, 59, 62, and 100: "What is your dominant state of life?," "What is your primary dissatisfaction (frustration)?," "What is your inner poison?," and "The role of sexuality in your balance: Sector VIII").

Native position

Position occupied in the astral chart by a planet at the time of birth. We will speak, for example, of "return to the natal or native position" when a planet, during its orbital revolution around the zodiac, returns to the place it occupies in the natal chart.

Sectors

Also called astrological houses, the sectors divide the zodiac wheel into twelve unequal portions, each part representing a domain of life. It is both important to nurture each of these areas (see p. 81, "Sectors, typical schedule"), but also to know how to give priority to one or the other according to the moments of life (see p. 131, "The right thing at the right time"), or to identify certain particularities of our psychology (see p. 100, "The role of sexuality in your balance: Sector VIII").

Signs of the zodiac

Symbolic division of the sky into twelve zones. When, as seen from the Earth, a planet passes through this area, we say it is in the corresponding sign. The signs were named according to the constellations present then, but it is important to note that the fact that these constellations have moved since then (precession of the equinoxes) has no impact, since it was just a matter of choosing a name to have a reference point. It is indeed the study of character as a function of the displacement of the planets in relation to the Earth (displacement that remains identical whatever the constellation in the background) that has made it possible to establish the laws of astrology.

If you are not sure of your astrological data:

You can obtain them free of charge on the author's website: www.autourdelalune.com

You can also download free software to calculate your own theme and that of your loved ones. Visit this site, which offers many of them: http://philipeau.free.fr/logiciels.htm

THE AUTHOR

Philippe Regnicoli has been passionate about astrology for more than 30 years. His interests include star symbolism and the importance of the stars in our lives. An astrologer for about 15 years, he's maintained the website AutourDeLaLune.com for 10 years, providing viewers around the world with a modern and practical vision of astrology. As the former general secretary of the Federation of French-Speaking Astrologers, Regnicoli regularly gives conferences in France, Switzerland, and Belgium.